KEY TO THE MISSAL

KEY

TO

THE MISSAL

Cornelius A. Bouman

AND

Mary Perkins Ryan

FIDES PUBLISHERS ASSOCIATION

NOTRE DAME, INDIANA

Library of Congress Catalog Number: 60-8447

Copyright: 1960, Fides Publishers Association, Notre Dame, Indiana

Nihil Obstat: Louis J. Putz, C.S.C.
University of Notre Dame

Imprimatur: Leo A. Pursley, D.D., Bishop of Fort Wayne, Indiana

Manufactured by American Book-Stratford Press
New York, New York

CONTENTS

INTRODUCTION

IF SOMEONE WERE to ask you, "What is the most important thing you do?" the right answer would be, "Take part in the holy sacrifice of the Mass." The Encyclical on the Sacred Liturgy says that this is "the chief duty and highest dignity" of every Christian.

Why is this? Because in the Mass, we who share Christ's life by baptism take part in His own supreme act of worship, His sacrifice of praise, which is also the sacrifice of our redemption.

This is why the Mass is the center of the Church's worship. We can understand it a little better if we call it "the celebration of the Holy Eucharist." "Mass" is not a very descriptive word; it originally referred to the last part of a church service, at the end of which the participants were formally dismissed. Then it came to be used for any church service, and soon for the service *par excellence,* the Holy Sacrifice. But the word "Eucharist" is more descriptive, for it refers to the center of the whole rite, the great prayer in which the Church fulfills the command that Christ gave His apostles at the Last Supper to "do this in memory of Me." He said a prayer of praise, adoration and thanksgiving over bread and wine and declared that they had become His body and blood, and then He gave this food and drink to His apostles to eat and drink.

This prayer was called "eucharistia," and the same name was given to the prayer the priest recites in which he repeats the narrative of the institution, following the instructions of the Lord. Thus, the name "Eucharist" came to be used for the whole rite.

Our Lord gave His apostles, whom He sent as He Himself had been sent by the Father, the power to "do this," and to transmit this power to their successors down through the ages. Bishops, in turn, share this power with their colleagues and co-workers, the priests. When the priest repeats our Lord's words and actions in celebrating the Eucharist, he is acting *in persona Christi,* in the very person of Christ. The Lord is present amongst us as He was at the institution in the Upper Room.

On that occasion, He did not speak simply of His body and blood; He spoke of His body as to be sacrificed, of His blood as to be shed for the multitude of men for the remission of sins, the blood of the new and eternal covenant between God and men. He referred to His coming Passion in such a way that this Passion was "sacramentally" present. And so, whenever the Eucharist is celebrated by the Church, the sacrifice of Calvary is present "sacramentally," but in full reality, so that the Church can offer it as her own.

This sacrifice is, above all, Christ's great act of adoration and praise of God's majesty. By His whole life on earth, but supremely by His passion and death, the incarnate Son translated into human terms, into human acts, the infinite praise that He offers eternally to the Father in the love of the Holy Spirit. When we take part in the Eucharist, we are taking part in this sacrifice of praise which Christ, the Head and High Priest of mankind, offers to God's majesty.

This sacrifice is, at the same time, the work of our redemption. In order to bring us with Him into God's presence, Christ's work of praise had to be a work of doing away with the obstacles that barred men from God—our sins. It had to be a work of overcoming sin and death, of undoing by His obedience the insult to God's majesty and the injury to human nature that had been wrought by the disobedience of Adam and of all sinful mankind. "By dying He destroyed our death and by rising again restored our life" (Easter Preface). Whenever the Holy Eucharist is celebrated this "whole work of our redemption is renewed" (Secret for Ninth Sunday after Pentecost). When we take part in the Holy Sacrifice, we ourselves are more fully redeemed, freed from sin, made holy and brought into the Father's presence by the power of Christ's passion and death. The whole Church is brought nearer to the full stature of her final perfection. The faithful departed share in its effects. The graces of salvation are poured out on the whole world.

The celebration of the Holy Eucharist is also the great act by which the Church witnesses to her Lord, "remembers" Him and His work. It is the act by which she "proclaims the death of the Lord until he comes" (1 Cor. 11:26) and thus proclaims her expectation of His coming in glory.

And, finally, Christ died to "gather together into one the children of God who were dispersed" (John 11:52). The celebration of the Eucharist is the chief means whereby the Church is built up, whereby her members are united ever more closely in the love of the Spirit. We cannot take real part in this sacrifice unless we are first reconciled with our brothers (Matt. 5:23). By taking part in it, we signify our willingness to become more and more "members of one body, we who partake of the one bread."

For our Lord did not simply make His body and blood present under the species of bread and wine: He added "Take and eat." As He had already told His disciples, "Unless you eat the flesh of the Son of Man and drink his blood, you shall not have life in you. . . . He who eats my flesh and drinks my blood, abides in me and I in him. As the living Father has sent me and as I live by the Father, so he who eats me, he also shall live by me" (Jn. 6:54-58). We do not fully take part in the celebration of the Eucharist unless we "take and eat."

Before taking part in the sacrifice that established the Old Covenant between God and His people on Mt. Sinai, the Israelites heard God's law read to them, the law that they were to live by, and they all accepted it before the sacrifice of the Old Covenant was offered. Before the institution of the Eucharist at the Last Supper, our Lord gave His apostles the new law of love—of love like His own—thus "fulfilling," giving to the Old Law a new dimension of love of God and neighbor. In the same way, from im-

memorial times, the Church has preceded the celebration of the Eucharist itself by a service centered
in the reading of God's Word, the law of our Christian lives.

And so in the Mass, there are set before us "the
two tables in the treasury of Holy Church. One table
is the sacred altar having the holy bread that is
Christ's precious body; the other is that of divine
law, containing holy teaching, instructing in right
faith, and leading steadily onward to the inner veil
where is the holy of holies" (*Imitation of Christ*, Bk.
IV, 11).

In the course of history, the Church in her wisdom has given form to this holy celebration with
varying readings, prayers and chants, according to
the feasts and seasons of the year. We find all these
put together in the Missal, the most important of
the books the Church uses in her worship.

The purpose of the following chapters is simply to
open out more fully to the reader the riches of this
"treasury of Holy Church."

CHAPTER 1 **HOW
OUR MISSAL
HAPPENED**

THE MISSAL IS A VERY SPECIAL KIND of book because
of what is in it and also because of how it was put
together. The best way to describe it is to call it the
master-script that gives the "speaking parts" to be
taken by the various people concerned in offering
the Holy Sacrifice.

This master-script did not fall from heaven complete. It is the result of some sixteen hundred years
of celebrating the Mass, from the evening of the Last
Supper until the year 1570 when the first official Roman Missal was published and its use introduced
into all the dioceses of the Church in the West. Its
origins go back even further than the time of our
Lord, to the prayer of the people of God in the Old
Testament.

At the Last Supper, as the celebrant recounts at
every Mass, our Lord "giving thanks, blessed" the
bread and wine and transformed them into His body

1

and blood offered in sacrifice. He did not read the
words of His thanksgiving-blessings out of a book,
but He did follow an established pattern for
meal-prayers. Scholars tell us that such meal-prayers
were customary among the Jews of our Lord's time,
not only in families, but also when a religious
teacher—"rabbi," as he was called—ate together with
his followers, his disciples.

In these prayers, devout Jews "blessed," that is,
praised and thanked, God for all that He is, and for
all He had done for His people, creating them, redeeming them from slavery in Egypt, making them
His own, protecting them, and blessing the earth so
that it produces food and drink. And they asked
that, having done so much in the past, He would
complete His work by fulfilling all the promises
made to their fathers and by establishing the kingdom of the Messiah.

These prayers of blessing were not written down
in fixed formulas. The father of the family or the
rabbi improvised them, though always following the
same general pattern. The apostles must often, before the Last Supper, have heard our Lord offer such
"blessings." [1]

His prayers at the Last Supper were, then, quite
traditional. And yet they were entirely new. The
traditional prayer-form praised God because of His
mercies in the past and for today's food, often refer-
ring to the banquet in the future kingdom of the
Messiah. Now this kingdom had come. Our Lord's
prayer at the Last Supper established the New Covenant in His blood with all men who would wish to
enter into it. He changed the Old Testament into

the reality of the New and fulfilled all desires by offering the new and eternal sacrifice of His death on the cross.

When the apostles came to "do this in memory of me," they followed the traditional pattern of the blessings that our Lord had used, as He had remade them. And, for several centuries, while each celebrant followed the same pattern in offering the great Eucharistic Prayer, he improvised the phrases.

But, as one would expect, some bishop's way of improvising would be better than another's, and a famous bishop's form of Eucharistic Prayer would be followed more or less exactly by his admirers and successors. Gradually, the set forms of the Eucharistic Prayer which are used in the Church today came to be formulated and set down in writing. These are called *anaphoras* in most non-Roman rites, and in our Roman rite are the various Prefaces and the Canon.[2]

As time went on, these formulas for the great Eucharistic Prayer, with its seasonal variations, began to be collected in volumes called Sacramentaries, for the use of the celebrating bishop or priest. Such volumes also contained the other varying prayer-formulas he would need at Mass: the Collect, the prayer over the offerings (Secret) and the prayer after Communion.[3] And, later various private prayers for the celebrant to say for his own devotion in the course of the Mass (for instance, the offertory prayers) were also included. These Sacramentaries, or books for the celebrant, are one of the sources of our Missal.

Long before the Eucharistic Prayer began to be
fixed and written down, another book was needed—
the book of the Scriptures. The chief community
service of the Jews of our Lord's time was the synagogue service on the Sabbath. Here the Scriptures
were read according to a definite order during the
year, and commented on by the head of the synagogue or a visiting rabbi.[4] The first Christians—devout Jews—went to their local synagogue on the
Sabbath (Saturday) for this prayer-service and then
met together for the Christian Eucharist on the
Lord's Day (Sunday). But—so early in the history of
the Church that scholars are not sure just when it
happened—a prayer-service along the lines of the
Jewish one was transferred to the Lord's Day and,
ordinarily, held as the preparation for the Eucharist.
What was read included not only the Scriptures of
the Old Testament, but the collected sayings of
Christ and accounts of His life and work, and letters
from the chief apostles. And these were gradually
formulated and written down under the inspiration
of the Holy Spirit to form the Scriptures of the New
Testament.

A book of readings from Scripture was, therefore,
needed at Mass, that is, a Lectionary, either the complete Scriptures with the places marked for each day,
or a collection of the selections actually used. This
book was for the use of the reader, or lector, and of
the deacon who proclaimed the Gospel.

One more element of our Missal is the Antiphonary, or collection of psalm verses to be sung
during Mass. The Psalms were sung by the people

of God of old, in liturgical worship in the temple, in the synagogue, in family and community prayers. And so the new people of God, the Church, sings them also, taking the word that God has given her and making it also her response to Him. Psalm verses, varying according to the season or feast, came to be used in the Mass for the Introit or entrance hymn; for the Gradual and Tract, both chants of meditation between the readings, and the verse with the biblical refrain, Alleluia, which might be interpreted here as a joyful hailing of Christ who comes among His people in the holy Gospel; for the Offertory hymn when the gifts of bread were placed on the altar,[5] and for the Communion procession. These chants were, little by little, collected in one book called the Antiphonary or Graduale, for the use of the cantors or singers.

During several centuries, Mass was celebrated with the various officials concerned using these different collections. (No book was needed for the people, because their part, like ours today, was short and simple, and nearly always the same.) [6] But with the spread of low Masses, the growing lack of understanding of Latin, and the decline of popular participation, the celebrant began to take over the readers' parts and the cantors' and even some of the people's, while the servers took over the rest. In those times this was obviously a necessity at low Mass, but the confusion of roles spread over to high Mass also. Even at a solemn high Mass, when there are special ministers to sing the readings and a choir to sing the chants, the celebrant says these parts too.[7]

Obviously, the celebrant would have had quite a

time trying to find the right places in several different books. And so, during the Middle Ages, Missals, or complete Mass-books, began to be put together. But there was still no exact uniformity.

This lack of regulation led to abuses in various places and to a great deal of confusion—which the Reformers were not slow to make capital of. And so the Council of Trent ordered that a uniform Missal be prepared, printed and published as the official Mass-book for all Masses of the Roman Rite, with some few exceptions. This was published in 1570, by authority of St. Pius V, and this is the Missal we use today. Many single feasts have been added since; but there was no major change from 1570 on, until the Revised Holy Week Rites were issued by the Holy See in 1956.[8]

The Missal, as we have it today, is divided into various sections. One is the "Ordinary," that is, the prayers and rites of the Mass which do not vary from one season or feast to another. In the official Missal (and in those for the faithful which follow the same arrangement), the Ordinary is found near the middle of the book, as being the most convenient place to open the book at.

In the other sections of the Missal, a group of Mass Propers, that is, the varying readings, prayers and chants for one Mass are brought together, the most important being the group called the Proper of the Time, and the next that called the Proper of the Saints. In this respect, too, the Missal has quite a history.

The first place, and rightly so, is occupied by the Proper of the Time. This mainly consists in the

Masses for the Sundays throughout the year, which form, as it were, the backbone of the Missal. The Sunday is the oldest feast of the Church, for the regular celebration of the Eucharist began with the custom of celebrating Mass very early on Sunday morning, thus holding a weekly celebration of Easter (that is, of the whole mystery of salvation) at the very hour of Christ's Resurrection. (This weekly celebration of Easter is, apparently, even older than the yearly celebration.)

Our Sunday was "the first day of the week" according to the Jewish scheme, the Sabbath, our Saturday, being the seventh. Since the Lord arose from the dead on this first day, it was—even as early as in the Apocalypse—called "the day of the Lord," and the new Israel, the Church, took over the old Sabbath, and gave it a new meaning. The old Sabbath was a "day of rest" celebrating God's accomplishing His work of creation. The day of the Lord is centered around the sacrifice which carried out God's work of re-creation, the work for which the first creation was only the preparation. The Lord's Day hallows our present life, made up of weeks and months and years, and is also a foretaste of the eternal day of the Lord and of the heavenly banquet. So the Fathers were fond of saying that this was not only the first day of the week, but the eighth, a day out of human time, opening out on life everlasting.

Very soon in the early centuries of the Church, Easter, the *annual* celebration of the whole mystery of salvation became the Sunday of Sundays. And gradually around it developed a whole cycle of holy days. The preparation for Easter extended to the forty days of Lent; the Easter season included the fifty days up to Pentecost. In the fourth century, the feast of the Nativity of our Lord began to be celebrated, and later secondary feasts and a season of preparation grew up around it. So the Proper of the Time in our present Missal gradually came into existence.

The Proper of the Saints developed rather differently. In the early Church, it became customary to celebrate the anniversaries of martyrs' deaths (called, very beautifully, their *natale* or birthday into eternal life) by celebrating Mass in the sanctuaries built over their tombs. These celebrations were, in time, taken over by other churches. Some major feasts in honor of the holy Mother of God, and of the apostles, likewise began in one particular place and spread widely. During the centuries, feast after feast has been added—and is still being added—to the calendar of the saints, so much so that at various times the authorities of the Church have had to step in to prevent these celebrations from overwhelming the Proper of the Time.

Sometimes one saint's Proper Mass was borrowed for the celebration of another saint, for whom the same texts seemed suitable. Thus, the Common of the Saints, found toward the end of the Missal, gradually developed, with Masses for martyrs, confessors, and so on. In the same way, collections of Mass Propers for special needs, of Masses for the dead and votive Masses, were included.

Our present Missal then, is one of the great sourcebooks of Catholic faith and devotion. From it we learn how the Church always has prayed; we learn how, through the centuries, the essential lines of her worship and prayer have developed; we learn how the Church prays today and would have us pray with her as her members.

For study and discussion: Compare any available Missals published for the use of the faithful. How do they differ in contents, arrangement? What do you think an ideal Missal for your use should contain in the way of introductions, explanatory notes and so on? What are some of the reasons why a Missal is almost indispensable today to a Catholic who wishes to live and pray with the Church? How does the way the Missal was made up help us to see how we should use it?

NOTES

1   Each rabbi must have had his own characteristic style of improvising these prayers—just as a priest, minister or rabbi today has his own style of giving the invocation opening an assembly or banquet. The disciples at Emmaus may well have "recognized" our Lord "in the breaking of bread" (Luke 24:30-31) by His characteristic style of blessing-prayers.

2   *Preface* does not mean *Introduction*. Scholars are not agreed as to the exact derivation of the Latin word *praefatio,* but it is generally thought to have been a technical term taken over from pagan worship and meaning a prayer "spoken out" by the priest while performing some sacred action. At one time, the term was applied to the whole Canon as well as to what is now called the Preface. In any case, we should remember that Preface and Canon together make up the core of the Mass, the great Eucharistic Prayer.

3   See pp. 14-15 for the function of these prayers. The Sacramentaries also contained other priestly prayers: for the administration of the sacraments, blessings, etc.

4   See Luke 4:15-31.

5   The faithful brought up gifts of bread and wine, a part of which was used for the Sacrifice, the rest being used for the support of the clergy and for the poor. It seems that they brought various gifts of food and drink and even other things. Our modern collection of money, taken up at this time in the Mass, serves the same purpose—enabling us to provide the materials for the Sacrifice, and for the support of the clergy and the good works of our parish and diocese.

6   These were: *Kyrie eleison;* the responses, primarily those in the dialogue before the Eucharistic Prayer and the Amen at the end of this prayer; the *Sanctus,* as the people's contribution to the act of praise before the Consecration; and often, it seems, the *Gloria Patri* after the psalm of the Introit, and the refrain *Alleluia* before the Gospel.

7   The new "Order" of the Holy Week rites issued in 1956 began the work of properly redistributing the roles among the various participants. Here the celebrant does not read the readings to himself; he sits and listens to the lector or deacon. The basic responses are indicated as the proper part of all the faithful present. The Instruction on Sacred Music and the Sacred Liturgy of Sept. 3, 1958, carried on the same work, indicating what are the "speaking parts" of the faithful, and various stages whereby they are to go about taking them. It also clearly indicates the function and the parts of the choir.

8   Even from this brief sketch, it is obvious that the liturgy of the Church has remained essentially the same through the centuries in its divinely instituted elements: the Word of God, the essential pattern of the Eucharistic Prayer which contains the Sacrifice, and Communion. But it has changed and developed in response to the varying outlook and needs of different times and different cultures. Many suggestions have been made during the last decades by responsible authorities—scholars and pastors of souls—as to possible further developments in our Mass rite which would bring out the basic structure of the Mass more

clearly for all to see, and make it easier for us to take our full part in it. The Holy See has frequently approved this work of scholarship, and we may hope that in our time, those suggestions will be acted on which will most fully "bring the Mass to the people" (Pius XII) and the people to the Mass.

CHAPTER 2 **HOW**

TO USE

THE MISSAL

I<small>F WE WANT TO LEARN</small> how to use the Missal to the
best advantage, we need to have a clear idea of what
we are using it for and what this implies. Obviously,
we want to use it to help us take our part in the
Holy Sacrifice as fully and fruitfully as possible.
What does this mean?

In Christian worship, God has the primary part.
It is He who takes the initiative, calling us together,
speaking to us, bowing down to us to lift us up to
His own divine level. Our part consists in allowing
Him thus to lift us up to Himself, and in actively
praying. All this takes place "in Christ our Lord."
As the Father bends down to us in His incarnate
Son, so we raise ourselves to Him in and through
Christ. This is true of our active part in worship too.
Christ is always there to pray together with us; when-
ever we pray, we pray through Him.

As a member of Christ's Mystical Body, each

Christian who is in God's grace is always united with the Head of that body. And so he is always in some way united with his fellow-members. His prayer is always offered through Christ, and his prayer always vibrates throughout the entire community of the Church. It is always somehow a prayer in behalf of the whole Church. Christian prayer is, therefore, never entirely "private"; it is essentially social. This is the reason why our assembling together to pray, our praying with the same thoughts and desires, using the same words and uniting the very sound of our voices, is such a wonderful expression of our belonging together in the Mystical Body. When we pray together, we experience our union with one another as children of the new and spiritual Israel, the *familia Dei,* the household of God which Christ acquired as He was dying on the cross.

But this does not mean that all prayer has to be prayer of this fully social kind. On the contrary, when we study the history of the liturgy, we discover more and more clearly that even in her official worship the Church leaves plenty of room for private prayer, for praying in our own words or without any words, and that the true Christian tradition consists in a harmony of corporate and private prayer.

What is worship, what is prayer? Rightly understood, it is above all the praise of God. Here too, God must come first. If we analyze the prayer that Christ Himself taught us, the Our Father, we see that the whole first half is praise; only in the second part do we begin to "ask" for ourselves.[1] And so our active part in the central and chief act of Christian worship, the Holy Sacrifice, is chiefly to give praise,[2] in, with and through Christ, and, in the second place, to ask our Father—again "through Christ our Lord"—for what we need.

The ideal way of using a Missal, then, is the way that best helps *you* to hear God speak, to realize His bowing down to you to take you to Himself; the way that best helps you to enter into the rhythm of corporate and private prayer laid out by the liturgy; the way that best helps you take your part in the praise and petition that the Church offers to God in and with her Head in the celebration of the Holy Sacrifice.

There is, then, no "one way" of using a Missal. Nevertheless, certain general principles can be indicated to help work out the best way for you.

1. Obviously the less you have to read, and the less you have to turn back and forth from Ordinary to Proper, the better. Reading at top speed to "keep up" with the priest is not helpful to prayer of any kind, and neither is turning pages.

2. In order to take our full part in the Mass, we *need* to read the parts that are meant to be *listened to* and those that we are meant *to take part in, if otherwise*, we could not hear and understand them.

The parts that we are meant *to listen to* are those in which God speaks to us His assembled people, through the living voice of the Church, that is, the Lesson (if any), the Epistle and the Gospel.[3] Our reading here is a substitute for hearing God's message proclaimed to us in a language we can understand. (But when the Epistle and Gospel are read to us in English, why not listen instead of reading?)

The prayers that we *are to take part in* are of

three different kinds: first, those that the celebrant prays in our name: the Collect, the prayer over the offerings (Secret), the great Eucharistic Prayer, the Our Father, the Post-Communion prayer. We need to read the three of these that are in the Proper— the changing Collect, Secret and Post-Communion, and also the changing Preface which opens the great Eucharistic Prayer (usually placed in the Ordinary) as a substitute for following what the priest is say-ing, since most of us do not understand Latin. As for the rest of the Eucharistic Prayer, the Canon, our work here is, above all, to offer Christ, and ourselves with Him, in His sacrifice of praise to the Father. It is much better to become familiar with the line of thought of the Canon, and then pray along that line without reading, than to spend this most sacred part of the Mass in hurried catching-up.[4]

The second kind of prayers we are to take part in are the varying chants of the Mass: the Introit, Grad-ual, Offertory and Communion verses, also found in the Proper. Ideally, we should be hearing these sung so that we could understand and enter into their thoughts and spirit, while singing short responses ourselves between verses. Our reading these in the Missal is a substitute.

And the third kind of prayers we are to take part in are those that make up our own "speaking part": the short responses by which we unite ourselves with the celebrant *before* he speaks and acts in our name, and by which we give our assent to what he *has* done and said; the short, unvarying chants—Kyrie, Gloria, Sanctus, Agnus Dei—by which we express together our praise of Christ and the Father; the Our Father (when this is said by the congregation at a low Mass) and the Creed.[5] Certainly anyone who has sung or said the short responses aloud for a few months does not need to read them out of a book. Only a little effort and trust in one's memory eliminates too the need for reading our other speaking parts.

3. This means that you *do need to read all the Proper parts* of the Mass (though not the Epistle and Gospel if these are read in English). But you do *not need to read anything in the Ordinary except the Preface.* Anything more than this should be read only in so far as necessary to help your memory (for your "speaking part"), your devotion and your own deep personal prayer and self-offering.

St. Pius X inaugurated the great work of bringing the faithful back to the "primary and indispensable source of the true Christian spirit—active participation in the sacred mysteries and in the public and solemn prayer of the Church." He made available to the faithful, as it had not been for centuries, that major aspect of participation: sharing in the banquet, receiving Communion. He fostered better religious instruction. He urged and promoted the external means of participation: singing by the faithful of their responses and other proper parts. His successors have carried on his work, clarifying the status of the faithful in the Church and their part in her life and worship.

During the same period, a great work of scholarship has been going on, bringing more clearly to light the basic structure of the Mass, the proper roles of the various participants, the function of the various rites and prayers. And the work of biblical as well as liturgical scholars is making the riches of the liturgical texts available to ordinary Christians, so that both the "Bread of the Word" and the "Bread of the Eucharist" may nourish our life in Christ as we take part in the worship of the Church.

We Catholics today, then, have a wonderful opportunity to "worship in spirit and in truth," if we take the trouble to prepare ourselves to do so. This means, among other things, that we take a few moments, toward the end of each week and before major feasts, to read through the Proper of the Mass for the coming Sunday or feast, and to think about it, in order to prepare our minds and hearts to take full part in that Mass. In the same way, we give the graces of the Mass a chance to fructify in our minds by using the liturgical texts as a basis for prayer and meditation during the following day or week.[6]

During the remaining chapters of this book, then, we shall study the main themes of each season and great feast of the Church as these are given us in the Propers of the Masses, to see how we may most fully enter into the Church's praise and prayer, and how we can best cooperate with her yearly program of formation so as to "grow up in all things in Christ, our Head," so as to make our whole lives that "spiritual sacrifice" which is the fruit of our taking part in the Mass on earth, and our preparation for taking part in the everlasting praise of God in heaven.

For study and discussion: How often is praise mentioned in the Ordinary, and in the Proper for next Sunday? How often "through Christ our Lord"? Make an outline of the prayers of the Mass, both Ordinary and

Proper, as they occur, indicating where you need to use the Missal, where not. Does your present method of using a Missal need any revision in order to make it a better tool for your taking part in the Church's worship?

NOTES

1   This may seem obvious, but it is also obvious that, for too many Christians, "to pray" means "to ask" and only this. Such a misapprehension is not of recent growth. Our English word "pray" is taken from the Latin *precari* which has the meaning only of "asking (God) a favor." We have no general term available which includes all kinds of prayer, as does the Latin *orare*.

2   Recent studies go to prove that the word "Eucharist" from the Greek, and the Latin *"gratias agere"* which are usually translated by "thanksgiving" and "giving thanks" respectively, were both translations of a Hebrew word with a much wider meaning, centered in the idea of praising, blessing, "confessing" God, with "thanksgiving" in the narrow sense as only one of its connotations.

3   Hearing the word of God proclaimed in the Church and by the Church, and responding to it in faith, is a basic activity of the Christian life as such. "Blessed are they who hear the word of God and keep it." By hearing the Epistle and Gospel at Mass together with the other texts of Scripture given us in the liturgy, we receive the word in its rightful Christian context, and learn how to hear it rightly and fruitfully in our own reading and prayer.

4   To understand the main line of thought in the Canon, we need to see it as basically the great prayer of praise which incorporates Christ's words and acts of institution at the Last Supper. Into this prayer of praise have been interwoven various other prayers asking the grace of the Sacrifice for the whole Church.

The main line of the prayer begins with the Preface, praising the Father, especially for some one of His wonder-

ful works for our salvation, and offering Him our praise
through Christ our Lord. With the Sanctus, we unite our
voices in this praise, together with those of all the heavenly
hosts. (Then several prayers have been interwoven asking
for the grace of the Sacrifice for the Church, the Pope, our
Bishop, all priests, all present . . . in communion with the
holy ones in heaven; and a prayer asking God to accom-
plish in our midst the "great deed" of the Consecration.)
The narrative of the institution then begins, making present the Sacrifice of Christ, which the whole Church, in the
prayer after the Consecration, offers as her own. (Then
there is a prayer for the graces of Communion, a prayer
that the faithful departed may also share in the joys of the
heavenly banquet in which we are going to partake in anticipation by Communion; and a prayer for the celebrant
and his assistants.) Lastly the Church acknowledges with joy
that everything comes to us from the Father through Christ,
and offers her sacrifice and praise through Him—by whom,
with whom, and through whom, all honor and glory are
given to the Father in the Spirit. And we all respond with
the "Great Amen" before the Our Father.

5   All the responses said by the servers are included in the
various stages of active participation outlined in the Instruction of Sept. 3, 1958. These include the long responses
in the prayers at the foot of the altar, and the response to
the Orate Frates, the Suscipiat. But these are not easy for
the average congregation to say and, historically, were not
designed to be prayers for the people. If the congregation
you belong to is saying these, fine—and otherwise if you
can read them without too much hurry, fine also. But it is
better to read the Introit prayerfully and omit the prayers
at the foot of the altar if you can't do both.

In the so-called "Community Mass," an English hymn
is sung as an entrance hymn, another at the Offertory, and
one while Communion is being distributed, to express in
common song the general ideas and sentiments appropriate
to these parts of the Mass. This is by way of substitution
for the more complex Proper of the Introit, Offertory and

Communion. The value of this practice in fostering com-
munal participation and basic ideas about the structure of
the Mass is obvious. But it is also true that no hymns, even
literary and musical masterpieces, can equal the words of
Holy Scripture itself. Singing hymns at these places in the
Mass is not the final stage of participation.

The arrangement of the unvarying chants of the Mass in
our chant books under the title of "Mass of the Angels,"
"Mass XVI," etc., might give the impression that these
chants make up some kind of unit and are all equally important, and, consequently, that in learning to recite or
sing them a congregation should begin with the Kyrie, take
up the Gloria next, and so on. But this is not true. The
congregation should begin with the Sanctus, since by saying
or singing it, the faithful take their part in the Great
Prayer which is the nucleus of the Eucharist proper. The
Kyrie and the Creed are next in importance, since these
have historically always belonged to the people's part. The
Gloria and the Agnus Dei can be mastered later, since, in
earlier times, these were often rendered by trained choirs
rather than by the people.

6   To make such prayer and meditation more fruitful, it is
well to read the complete Psalm from which the Introit,
Gradual, etc., are taken, and to study the Epistle and Gospel
in the context of the whole chapters of Scripture from which
they have been excerpted.

CHAPTER 3   ADVENT

To UNDERSTAND ANY SEASON of the liturgical year,
but especially Advent,[1] we need to understand the
perspective from which the Church views human
history, past, present and future. The idea that time
and human history are getting somewhere—not just
going round in circles, but aiming towards some
goal—gives history its real sense. This is how we see
history in its true dimension, that is, in its connection with God's eternal plan—a plan of divine mercy
—in short: the history of salvation.

The history of the Chosen People of old is the history of growing hope, of looking forward more and
more eagerly to the time when God would send the
promised Redeemer, who would bring judgment
against God's enemies, salvation and peace to His
faithful servants. As the prophets of the Old Testament looked forward to the fulfillment of God's
promises, they saw it all as one whole: the coming

of the Redeemer, His work, and the final accomplishment of that work. As one sees a city in the distance all at one glance, without discerning all the details and without perceiving that some high buildings are actually much further away than is the suburb in the foreground, so the prophets saw the times of the Messiah as one day opening out on eternity, without discerning clearly between the kingdom as it would be on earth (the Church) and the eternal kingdom in heavenly glory.

When Christ our Lord was born, those new times began, and we are living in them today. These are the "years of the Lord." [2] But His coming was not only the fulfillment of God's promises and of human hopes. It was also the promise of the full revelation in the future of what is now present and real, it is true, but still hidden from us. Christ is with us now, our Emmanuel (God-with-us). He is carrying out His redeeming work in and through the Church. We are called to be His messengers and instruments to bring His salvation to the ends of the earth. But we are still living by faith and looking forward to the final accomplishment of His work, to His visible coming in glory at the end of the world, when our faith will be changed into "seeing." His coming at the first Christmas was the dawn; the years of Christian history are the years of the continual coming of His light; His coming at the end of the world will bring the full daylight of eternal life.

The Masses of Advent can seem very confusing if we do not understand this Christian view of "what time it is," here and now, in this year of the Lord. For the liturgy speaks now of Christ's coming at the last day, now of His coming by grace in His Church, now of His coming at His birth in Bethlehem. And often the liturgy alludes to these various comings all at the same time, since they are all viewed in one single perspective.

During Advent, then, we are preparing to celebrate the anniversary of His birth, in which He will come to us with His grace, as the pledge and foretaste of His final coming in glory. These three comings are the three phases of His one great coming to men to bring men to God.

It is because the historic Israel, God's people and prophets of old, looked forward to the coming of the Redeemer as one complete whole, that we, so many centuries later and after the birth of Christ, can make their thoughts and hopes and desires our own. The Church does not want us to make believe that we are back in the times before the coming of Christ. We are the "Israel of the Spirit," the new people of God, for whom the great hope of the Israel of old has been realized, and yet intensified. But it is the same hope. And we learn from the thoughts and longings of the holy men and women of old what our own should be.

During this season, the Church puts before our eyes three great servants of the Lord: Isaias, the prophet who spoke most clearly about the coming of the Messiah [3] and His work, and about the universality of His salvation. St. John the Baptist, whom our Lord called "a prophet and more than a prophet," the last and greatest of all, who was privileged to "prepare the way of the Lord" in the hearts of His People and actually to point Him out as present among them: "Behold the Lamb of God." And, lastly, the holy Mother of God, the "daughter of Israel," representing all those who belonged to the people of Israel, in whom all their hopes were focussed, in whom they were fulfilled.[4]

Isaias shows us especially the eager joy with which we should prepare for the Lord's coming. St. John the Baptist shows us the need for complete "conversion," that is, for turning completely to God, and the "penance" which is an essential part of this turning. And the Mother of God shows us that our preparation for Christ's coming is to consist, above all, in complete acceptance of God's plan and His will and in confident praise of His mercy and of His faithfulness to His promises.

The Church puts four psalms in particular on our lips during this season: 24, 84, 79, and 18. Psalm 24 expresses our trust in God: "Of all who await you, not one shall be disappointed"; and our longing to have Him show us what He wants of us: "Show me, O Lord, your ways; teach me your paths." Psalm 84 praises God for what He has already done for us, and prays for His more complete coming, for the fullness of redemption: "Show us, O Lord, your mercy and grant us your salvation. . . . Yes, his salvation is near at hand for those who fear him, that the glory may dwell in our land." Psalm 79 prays for the coming of the Shepherd of Israel to give life to His sinful but repentant people.

Psalm 18, which we begin to use towards the end of Advent, sings the way in which the majesty of the visible heavens, ordered by God, gives praise to Him; in the same way, His law, invisibly ordering our lives, causes us to praise Him also. Christ, who is God's law of love in person, is the Light of the World, the Sun of Justice. He espoused our human nature in the Virgin's womb. And so the Church delights to apply two lines of this psalm to His human birth, when He entered upon His redeeming work: ". . . like the sun who comes out of his chamber like a bridegroom, exulting like a champion to run his course."

In the Gospel of the First Sunday of Advent, our Lord describes the end of the world in a prophecy that shows the destruction of Jerusalem (which took place a few decades after His Ascension) and the end of the world in one perspective. The destruction of the earthly city of Jerusalem meant the end of the old order and the beginning of Christ's coming to all mankind in the power of His grace through His Church. And so it was the sign of His final coming "on the clouds of heaven, in great power and majesty" at the end of the world. Those who have opposed God's kingdom will then "wither away with fear." But for those who have prepared for Christ's return, the full revelation of redemption is at hand.

Thus, on this same First Sunday, we pray for Christ's present coming in His grace: "Arouse your power, O Lord, we pray, and come: that, from the threatening perils of our sins, with you to protect us, we may be rescued; with you to free us, we may be saved."

The Gospel of the Second Sunday gives us our

Lord's praise of His forerunner, St. John the Baptist, "of whom it was written: Behold, I send my messenger ahead of you, who is to prepare your path before you come." The Collect prays that we may carry out in our own times the work of St. John: "Arouse, O Lord, our hearts, to prepare the paths of your only Son; so that, by his coming, we may be able to serve you with minds made pure."

The Gospel of the Third Sunday gives us St. John's own description of his mission: to be "the voice of one crying in the wilderness, make straight the way of the Lord!" In the Collect, we ask: "We pray you, O Lord, give a hearing to our prayers, and bring light into the darkness of our minds by the grace of your coming."

The Gospel of the Fourth Sunday locates the beginning of Our Lord's work on earth in its historic perspective. "In the fifteenth year of the reign of the emperor Tiberius . . . the word of the Lord came to John. . . . And he went into all the country around. . . . Prepare the way of the Lord." And so we pray for His ever fuller coming with His grace and for His final coming in glory: "Arouse your power, O Lord, we pray, and come: come to our aid with your great power; that, through the help of your grace, what our sins are delaying may be hastened by your merciful forgiveness."

So, from these Advent Masses, we learn how to prepare for Christ's coming by our prayer. And we also learn how to prepare for it by everything we do. St. Paul tells us very clearly in the Epistles for the four Sundays: "Walk in the light"; "Put on the Lord Jesus Christ"; "Support one another after

Christ's own example." We are to live in such a way that the very sight of how we act will show that the Lord is near. "Let your well-ordered way of life be visible to all men: the Lord is near." We are to be faithful servants, charged with ministering to others the mysteries of God's love.

Let us, then, so take part in the Church's preparation for Christmas during the holy season of Advent that we can whole-heartedly pray the Collect prayer on the Vigil of Christmas: "O God, as you make us glad with the yearly expectation of our redemption; grant that we who now joyfully receive your only Son as our Redeemer, may also without fear behold him coming as our Judge."

For study and discussion: In the Gospel of St. Luke, read Mary's song, the Magnificat, and that of the father of St. John the Baptist, (Canticle of Zachary). How do these songs apply to our Lord's earthly life? To His coming in the Church? To His future coming in glory and our life with Him in the world to come?

NOTES

1 The idea that the first Sunday of Advent is the "New Year's Day" of the Church is not entirely correct. In the Roman-dominated civilization of the first Christian centuries, the new year began when our own does—our calendar is still basically the same as theirs—around the time of the winter solstice, when the days stop getting shorter and begin to lengthen again. This was felt to be the annual re-birth of the sun's light, in some way supporting men's hopes that life and goodness are never completely overcome by death and evil. And so it seems the proper time to begin a new year of human time. The feast of Christmas was put at the same time of year for somewhat

the same reasons. And so, if there is any New Year's Day in the Church's calendar, it is Christmas Day (this is when, even today, Cardinals and Ambassadors go to present their New Year's wishes to the Holy Father). The season of preparation for Christmas was, apparently, given its present form at the time of St. Gregory the Great. And when the liturgical books came to be put together, it was natural that, in the long run, the texts of the preparation season came to be copied before those of Christmas. This is why the Missal now begins with the First Sunday of Advent.

2   The years before Christ's coming are simply numbered so many years "B.C." But we date events after His coming as happening in the _____ year of the Lord—*Anno Domini* 1960 or whatever.

3   *Messiah* is the English form of the Hebrew participle of which the Greek translation is *Christos,* meaning in English *The Anointed.* In the Old Testament, priests and kings received a solemn anointing as the sign of their being chosen by God for their offices and empowered by Him to carry them out. And so the promised Redeemer was to be anointed by the very Spirit of God to carry out His mission as High Priest and King.

4   As L. Bouyer points out in *The Meaning of Sacrea Scripture* (Notre Dame University Press, 1958), God's long education and training of His people throughout the Old Testament was, in spite of Christ's rejection by "the Jews," a complete success: pre-eminently in Mary; also in John the Baptist and in all those who, like Simeon and Anna, were faithfully "waiting for the consolation of Israel"; and in all those who did welcome Christ, the apostles and first Christians.

5   Advent is not a season of penance in the same sense as Lent, which is the great season of Christian warfare against the Enemy and his allies within each of us. Yet during Advent we are asked to heed St. John's call to "make ready the way of the Lord" in our own hearts.

CHAPTER 4 THE CHRISTMAS-
EPIPHANY
SEASON

THE CHRISTMAS LITURGY is filled with light. The
candles in our churches, on Christmas trees and in
windows, the lights that fill stores and city streets,
are only reflections of the splendor of light radiating
the Masses of this holy season. "O God, you have
made this holy night resplendent with the radiance
of the true light" (Midnight Mass). "Light has shone
out today on the whole world" (Dawn Mass).
". . . that we who are permeated with the new
light of your incarnate Word, may have this light
resplendent in our work which shines by faith in
our minds" (Prayer for Dawn Mass). "A holy day
illumines us . . . today a great light has come down
on our earth" (Day Mass).

And not only Christmas Day itself; the Preface
sung from Christmas to Epiphany carries on the
same theme: ". . . to give thanks to you . . . for,
through the mystery of the Word made flesh, the

new light of your brightness has shone out to the
eyes of our hearts."

The Epiphany Mass and Preface shine out with
the same radiance of Christ's light come down to
our earth: "Arise, be radiant, O Jerusalem; your
dawn has come and the glory of the Lord has risen
upon you. . . . The nations will walk in your light,
and kings in the brightness of your rising" (Lesson).
". . . to give thanks to you . . . for, when your only
Son appeared in the substance of our mortal nature,
he restored us by the light of his immortal nature"
(Preface).

The idea of God as light is as old as mankind
itself. When the Lord appeared to His people in the
Old Testament, His glory was the visible sign and
cloak of His unthinkable majesty. The Redeemer
whom God had promised comes to "bring light to
them who sit in darkness and the shadow of death."
He is to be the Sun of Justice, Light of the World.

This is the reason why the feasts of Christmas
and Epiphany were placed at this time of year. Nobody knows the actual day of the year on which
Christ was born. But what could be more fitting
than to celebrate the birth of the True Light in
our world at the time when the sun begins once
more to rise again in the heavens, when the days begin to lengthen and light triumphs over darkness? So, during the first half of the fourth century,
the feast of Christmas began to be celebrated in the
Western Church; and, even earlier, the Eastern
Churches had established the feast of the Epiphany.
In time, the East began to celebrate Christmas also;

and the West, Epiphany; and other feasts began to be established around these two. Now we have the "twelve days of Christmas" from Christmas to the Epiphany, and the Epiphany season goes on until Septuagesima.

But these two feasts are not duplications. Each of them brings out one great aspect of the phrase in which St. John sums up the mystery of the Incarnation: "The Word was made flesh and dwelt amongst us. And we saw his glory—glory of the only Son of the Father—full of grace and truth."

Christmas, and the feasts associated with it, bring out particularly the first aspect: the historic fact that the Word, the Son, the Light, took on our human nature in the Virgin's womb and was born as a human child, "like us in all things except sin." Once, when there was only one Christmas Mass, the whole second chapter of St. Luke, telling of our Lord's birth, His circumcision, His presentation in the Temple, His childhood in Nazareth and His finding in the Temple, was all read at that Mass.[1] Now we have various feasts using different sections of this Gospel to bring out different aspects of the same wonderful fact that God became man to bring men back to God, the Son of God took on our human nature to give us a share in His divine nature.[2] These feasts are: the Sunday within the Christmas Octave, its octave day (the Circumcision), the feasts of the Holy Name of Jesus, the Holy Family, and Candlemas Day on February 2.

The Epistles of these Masses teach us the implications for our own lives of this same mystery of God's love: how we should praise Him, how we should respond to Him with joy, how we should live lives worthy of the life that Christ came to give us. And the prayers ask for the graces we need to do this.

The chants of these Masses are taken mainly from the two prophetic Psalms, 2 and 109, singing of Christ's more than human dignity, His royal and universal rule, His priesthood; and from Psalms 95, 97, 99, and most frequently 92, all singing the joy of the world at God's coming; His power and His justice as He comes to rule the earth.

The Feast of the Epiphany, and the celebrations connected with it, bring out rather the second aspect of the mystery of Christ's coming amongst us: "We saw His glory, the glory of the only Son of the Father." Epiphany means "showing-forth," or "manifestation," and seems to have been used, in the Greco-Roman civilization of the first few centuries, as a technical term for the public appearance of the Emperor in some city. And so the same term was applied to the manifestation of the King of Kings in our midst—both in His human life and in His coming at the last day.

The Gospel of the feast itself proclaims Christ's manifestation to the Wise Men from the East, representatives of all mankind. Christ's salvation is not limited to the Jewish people, it is for the whole world. This is why Epiphany, and Pentecost, present us with the biblical-theological reasons for everything that the Church is doing in the field of home and foreign missions.

On the Sunday within the octave, the Gospel

tells us of our Lord's mysterious "showing" Himself to His parents as the Son of His eternal Father, at the finding in the Temple. The Gospel of the octave day gives His great manifestation as the Son of the Father and the promised Messiah when He was baptized in the Jordan; that of the following Sunday, His "manifesting His glory" to His disciples by His first miracle at the wedding-feast of Cana; and the Third and Fourth Sundays after Epiphany proclaim His showing His divine power and His mission of salvation by one or another "sign" or miracle.

The Epistles of these Masses bring out the same theme, developing its next stage: Christ is now manifesting Himself to all men through the Church, the new Israel "according to the Spirit." Christ shows us His glory here and now in the Church through the great wonders He does for us in the sacraments (an old name for baptism was "illumination"). We are to live so as to be the heralds and transmitters of His light, radiating it to the whole world, and the prayers of these Masses ask for the grace to carry out our task.

The chants for the Feast of the Epiphany itself are taken from Psalm 71, describing the royal rule of the Messiah, the king of justice and peace. Other psalms used during this time are: 88, praising God's majesty and His wonderful promises to the house of David, promises fulfilled in Christ; Psalm 44, the royal marriage-song, praising the greatness and power of the king and the beauty of His bride—figures of Christ and the Church; Psalms 65 and

106, praising God for His wonderful deeds of deliverance, and 117, the great Easter song of triumph.

Beginning with the Third Sunday after Epiphany, the chants of the Masses are always the same until the end of this season. Psalm 96, used in the Introit and Alleluia verse, is another "Epiphany" psalm, singing our joy at God's coming amongst us—in His earthly life, in the Church here and now, and in His visible glory at the end of the world. Psalm 101, in the Gradual, sings of God's rebuilding of Sion and revealing Himself there in His glory. Through all the centuries, Christ is building up His Church, to which some day the historic people of Israel will also return. Now He reveals Himself here invisibly to our faith; at the end of the world, He will reveal Himself in the eternal Church in His glory.

The Offertory chant is taken from Psalm 117, the Easter song of deliverance. Christ's coming on earth was the inauguration of the work of our redemption. The mystery of His Incarnation is one with the mystery of our redemption—as we sing in the Creed: "Who for us men and for our salvation, came down from heaven, and was made flesh of the Virgin Mary." The mystery we celebrate from Christmas to the end of the Epiphany season is the anticipation of the Easter mystery.

For study and discussion: Take one or more of the Epistles of this season. How does it teach us to live in our daily lives the mystery we are celebrating? Which psalm-verses from these Masses do you find especially appropriate for daily praise and prayer? Read as many as possible of the psalms used in the Masses. How does reading the whole psalm help you grow in awareness of the Christmas-Epiphany mystery?

NOTES

1 At first there was only one Mass on Christmas day. Gradually, the practice developed of celebrating our three present Masses, or rather four, since the Vigil Mass was once sung in the afternoon, when the feast actually begins. The Pope would keep vigil and celebrate the Night Mass, with his household and a few monks and devout lay-people, in the crypt of the basilica of St. Mary Major where a relic of the crib is preserved. In the morning, he sang a Mass at the small church of St. Anastasia, a martyr whose feast must have already been honored before Christmas was established on this day. When the Christian liturgy was given greater splendor, a new Proper, our present Dawn Mass, was composed. And, finally, the Pope celebrated the main Mass, our Day Mass, at St. Peter's. (Since the 11th century, this Mass is also celebrated at St. Mary Major, but at the altar in the great nave.) When the Roman liturgical books were introduced outside Rome and gradually penetrated into all the countries of Western Europe, these three Masses of the Pope's became a regular feature of the liturgy in every church.

2 The Secret of the Christmas Midnight Mass beautifully sums up this aspect of the "mystery of Christ": "May the offering of today's feast be acceptable to you, O Lord; so that by the abundant outpouring of your grace, through these holy exchanges *(sancta commercia)*, we may be found in the likeness of him in whom our substance is now with you." The Incarnation is a mystery of "exchanges"—God taking our manhood so that we may be lifted up to His divinity. He takes our life so that we may share in His life (for we are not only called God's children, St. John tells us, we are His sons in actual reality). In the "exchanges" of the

Holy Sacrifice, our gifts of bread and wine are transformed into Christ's body and blood offered in sacrifice to the Father, so that we may be transformed more and more completely into His likeness, by taking part in the sacrifice and receiving His gift.

CHAPTER 5 **PRE-LENT AND THE HOLY FORTY DAYS**

Septuagesima sunday, the Sunday that comes about seventy days before Easter, is a great turning-point in the liturgical year. We can tell this even from the externals of the liturgy: the priest and the altar are clothed in penitential purple; the Alleluia in the chants is silenced; no Gloria is said or sung. The Church turns our attention from the celebration of the mystery of Christ's coming in our nature and begins to prepare us to celebrate the mystery of the work He came to carry out in our nature—the work of the redemption.

The Introit of this Mass gives us the themes of this pre-lenten season: our misery, due to our sins; our need to cry out to the Lord; His power to save us. "The terrors of death flowed all round me, the sorrows of hell surrounded me: and in my anguish I cried to the Lord, and from his holy temple he heard my voice." We are now to meditate on what modern writers call "the human situation," the state into which mankind has been brought by sin; our share in this misery and in the responsibility for it. But when we make this meditation with the Church, it is not to lead us to despair, but rather to cry out to the Lord in trustful hope.[1]

Psalm 17, from which the Introit is taken, is David's great song praising God for all His wonderful acts of deliverance, foreshadowing the Resurrection of Christ from the dead and our own redemption. And so with the other chants of this Mass and of the two following Sundays: read the whole psalm from which each is taken, and you will find that each is a song about the deliverance of one of God's servants or of His whole people, a song of redemption already accomplished or hoped for— all foreshadowing Christ's victory over sin and death and our own victory in Him.

The Epistle of Septuagesima adds another theme, which also will continue throughout Lent. We are not to await God's redemption passively. We have to fight against God's enemies, the evil in ourselves above all. We have to work, and work hard, to co-operate with His grace. We must "run so as to obtain the prize." As athletes undertake privations and exercises to obtain a temporal reward, how much more should we for an eternal. The fact that we have been baptized and received the food of immortality does not mean that God is entirely pleased with us, any more than He was with the Israelites.

We must chastize our bodies so as to become good servants of Christ.

The Epistle of Sexagesima Sunday, the Sunday about sixty days before Easter (the Mass is in honor of St. Paul, whose church was the stational church of the day),[2] shows us that with Christ's grace we can even "glory" in the pains and distresses of our present life: "Gladly, then, will I glory in my weaknesses so that the power of Christ may dwell in me." And the Epistle of Quinquagesima shows us the power that Christ gives us to arrive at our goal: faith, hope, and charity.

The Gospels of Septuagesima and Sexagesima are part of a series which began on the Fifth Sunday after Epiphany, with the theme of Christ manifesting Himself in His Church. When this prelenten series was organized, these Gospels were retained in the Masses for these Sundays. And they fit in well here: Christ is calling *us to work* in His vineyard, even if all our lives so far we have been "standing about idle" (Septuagesima). The grain of the word which has been sown in our lives is for us to receive in the good soil of a true and generous heart, so as to "bring forth fruit in patience" (Sexagesima). A few days before Ash Wednesday, the Gospel announces our journey with Christ to His passion and death, and the cure of the blind man who then at once "followed Jesus" on His way.

Thus during this pre-lenten season, the Church gives us, so to say, the opening conferences preparing us for her great yearly retreat, the holy forty days.

Why forty days for this annual retreat? Because this is the length of time sacred throughout Scripture as a period of fasting and prayer in preparation for some great manifestation of God's power and mercy. Moses fasted and prayed for forty days before receiving the law from God on Mt. Sinai. Elias journeyed for forty days to Mt. Horeb where God revealed Himself to him. And, above all, Christ fasted for forty days in the desert before beginning His public ministry. From very early times, then, a period of forty days was established in which the whole Church makes ready by prayer and fasting to celebrate the mystery of Christ's redeeming death.

Originally, Lent began on what is now the First Sunday; at that time the Easter celebration was thought of as beginning on Holy Thursday. Later on, the forty days were reckoned from the Wednesday before the First Sunday of Lent, the day on which those who were to do public penance came to church to receive the outward token of their penitence, the blessed ashes. The days counted now are those of actual fasting, leaving out the Sundays. When this way of reckoning began, the unity of Christ's death and resurrection in the one work of redemption was no longer so clearly understood, so Holy Thursday, Good Friday and Holy Saturday were included in the Lenten season rather than in the Easter celebration.

What does the Church want us to do during the days of this retreat? In a sermon read in the Breviary on the First Sunday of Lent, St. Leo says that as Christians we should always be in that state of spiritual cleanliness and zeal fitting for the celebration of the mysteries of our redemption. But, alas, this is not so. The "dust of worldliness," of absorption in worldly interests, our weakness and sinfulness, render us unfit. The Church, therefore, gives us the special lessons and graces of these holy forty days in which to put us into the state we ought always to be in, the state to which we were raised by baptism. Or, as has also been pointed out, if we do not, like the religious, give the whole of our life to God, the Church invites us now at least to offer Him the tithes, one tenth, of the days of the year.

In the early Church, Lent was the great period of immediate preparation for baptism, which was given during the holy Easter night. Many of the liturgical readings and chants were chosen with a view to the instruction of the *baptizandi* and to their liturgical preparation, by exorcisms and the prayer of the Church, to take their part in the struggle against Satan needed in order to renounce him completely and to enter Christ's service.

Lent was also the season of carrying out public penance. Those who had sinned grievously and publicly, and had repented, were given a special program of fasting and prayer and public self-humbling so that they might be absolved and admitted to full membership in the Church to celebrate the paschal feast. The liturgy has many references to the need for penance, and to the marvelous answers that the mercy of God has granted, and always will grant, to those who truly repent and are "converted to the Lord."

We are now preparing for the renewal of the

grace of our baptism during the holy night; we are doing penance for our own sins, realizing our membership in the sinful race of men and our share in responsibility for the miseries and sins of all mankind. And so the lenten liturgy is for all of us, to give us God's message of hope, to cry out to Him for help with the whole Church.

How are we to "do penance" during these forty days? The lenten Masses, especially during the first four weeks, constantly remind us of the necessity for *fasting:* the necessity for physical fasting (and the rules of the Church are now so easy that almost everyone not actually ill can observe them; it is more a matter of attention than of physical hardship). And there is need also for the more difficult "fasting" from anything that goes against God's law, especially His law of justice and charity to others. Many of the Lessons of these Masses remind us that justice and kindness in all our dealings with one another are absolute prerequisites to pleasing God; that fasting from satisfying our own selfishness is the fast He really wants.

Another element, therefore, in our lenten penance is to be *almsgiving,* the giving to those in need of what we save by denying ourselves. (And this does not mean money only; it can mean time and energy as well—giving extra acts of thoughtfulness, works of kindness or sympathy or humor). For the life given us in baptism, the life in which we are to be renewed by taking part in the mysteries of our redemption at Easter, is, above all, a life lived in

God's Spirit of love, the love which is overflowing divine generosity.

The third element in our lenten preparation is *prayer*. We are engaged in a struggle, not with flesh and blood, but with the "powers of this world of darkness," with the evil within and outside ourselves. We humbly acknowledge that we cannot overcome the Evil One, nor the weakness, selfishness and sinfulness in ourselves, by our own efforts. Lent is the time for "calling out to God," humbly and trustfully asking His aid for ourselves, for the whole Church, for all mankind.

When we make this annual retreat with the Church, we are joining *with* the whole Church, with all her millions and millions of members all over the world. We share their effort; we make our small contribution to the whole. Better still, all this becomes the effort and prayer, not only of so many individual men, but also of the Bride of Christ. And it is, therefore, one with the redeeming work and prayer of Christ Himself, who took on all our pains and the burden of our sins, so as to bring us with Him to share His everlasting life and joy.

Questions for study and discussion. In your Missal, read the Blessing of the Ashes (before the Mass of Ash Wednesday). Find the passage of Genesis from which the phrase is taken that is said when the ashes are put on your forehead. What light does this shed on our lenten penance, and on its purpose of preparing us to celebrate the mystery of our redemption? Should one receive these ashes if one does not seriously intend to spend Lent as a time of prayer and penance? Make out a practical lenten program, including time to read and think about the lenten Masses (it is highly desirable to do this in order to receive the Church's lessons and to take part in her prayer, even if one cannot take part in the Mass every day).

NOTES

1   In the Office today, the Church begins to read the Book of Genesis—the story of creation, and of the Fall that came so soon to mar and warp what God had made "very good." But the account of the Fall includes also the promise of the Redeemer who will re-create all things in the paschal mystery.

2   The "station" was the church in or near Rome to which, in former times, the Pope went to celebrate the Mass of the day. Many of the Masses are designed with the particular stational church in mind. On some days, the custom of going in procession to the stational church and there singing a solemn Mass has been revived in our times.

CHAPTER 6 # THE SUNDAYS OF LENT AND PASSIONTIDE

THE SUNDAYS OF LENT AND PASSIONTIDE are like so many great steps by which we ascend to the celebration of the mystery of our redemption. During the weeks between, we carry on our work of prayer and penance, realizing more and more clearly our weakness and need for God's help. The Sundays of this holy season give us a breathing-space, an opportunity to see where we are going, to see what God is doing for us during Lent and what He promises us as the reward of our lenten efforts.

The Epistle of the *First Sunday,* originally the opening of Lent, tells us that "now is the time of grace, now is the day of salvation," now we are to show ourselves valiant servants of Christ, fighting with His weapons of holiness and love.

In the Gospel, we see our Lord Himself fasting for forty days and forty nights and then being tempted by the devil. We are given this highest motivation for our fasting—to become more like Christ—and we are shown where to look for strength to overcome the Tempter. In his sermon on this Gospel, read in the Office of the day, St. Gregory says that at first our minds shrink from the incredible thought that the sinless Son of God would allow Himself to be tempted by the Evil One. But then we realize that, since He was willing to die for us, it is not so surprising that He was willing also to be tempted for us. "For it was fitting that He should conquer our temptations by His, as He had come to overcome our death by His own."

In all the chants of this Mass, the Church uses Psalm 90, the very psalm quoted by the devil in tempting Christ to presume on God's loving protection in order to make things easy for Himself and His work: "He has entrusted you to His angels to guard you in all your ways; they shall lift you on their hands, lest you stumble on a stone." In His answer to this temptation, "Thou shalt not tempt the Lord thy God," Christ shows us how to understand this psalm and all those like it; He shows us what true trust in God is. We are not to presume that God will work miracles to save us from difficulties and trouble. Christ Himself was not to be spared the bitter "cup" of His Passion, but to go through suffering and death to the glory of His Resurrection. And we, following His example, are to trust humbly in God's power to save us, not *from* difficulties and troubles, but *through* them, by the power of Christ's death.

The *Second Sunday of Lent* shows us the glorious goal of all our striving—to share in Christ's glory. Shortly before His Passion, our Lord showed Himself to three of His apostles in the light of heavenly glory, with the witness of two great mystics of the Old Testament, Moses and Elias (representing the law and the prophets), and the testimony of the Father: "This is my beloved Son" and the solemn command to hear Him, our only teacher. This vision, the Fathers tell us, was to strengthen the faith of the apostles when they saw Christ undergoing the suffering and humiliations of His Passion. And so the Church gives us this Gospel early in Lent to build up our faith in Christ our teacher and our hope that if we share His sufferings now, we shall also share His glory in the life to come.

The *Third Sunday* shows us clearly, both in the Epistle and the Gospel, the choice that lies before us all our lives long—to serve God or to serve the Evil One; we cannot be neutral, this only leads to a more complete enslavement to the devil. We tend too easily today to feel that the Evil One has somehow been evaporated into psychoses and neuroses and maladjustments, that he doesn't really exist at all. But modern analyses of the weaknesses of human nature, most useful as they are, do not do away with the Evil One. Christ, who knows human nature in all its complexities, certainly thought that the devil existed, and so does His Church. Today's Gospel reminds us that we must be positively *for* Christ, if we are not to be on the devil's side. How do we do this? The Epistle tells us: by "living in love, accord-

ing to the example Christ gave us, He who loved us
even to delivering Himself for us, offering Himself
to God as a perfect sacrifice." And the Gospel tells
us, in our Lord's wonderful praise of His Mother:
"Blessed are they who hear the word of God and
keep it."

Laetare Sunday—so called from the first word of
the Introit—has, more than any other of the lenten
Sundays, the quality of refreshment, consolation, en-
couragement. Here in the middle of Lent, the
Church invites us to be glad, to look forward to the
joy that will be ours in heaven, the joy that is ours
here and now in the Church on earth, the joy that
will be renewed in our Easter celebration.

This Sunday gives a special Christian dimension
to the gladness that should be ours. The Epistle and
Gospel and the chants of the Mass are all about the
Church. She is the new Jerusalem, the city of God.
She is free, with the freedom of the very Spirit of
God which is her Spirit. And we her children are
free also. We have been delivered by Christ from
slavery to death and evil. We share in His freedom,
the liberty of children of God.

But this freedom is freedom to love, to love freely
and generously as God has loved us. It is the Holy
Eucharist, foreshadowed in the Gospel of the miracle
of the feeding of the five thousand, which is the
bond of our unity of life and love in the Church.
It is the Eucharist which builds us up into "one
body, all who partake of the one bread." So this
Sunday looks forward to Holy Thursday, to the
proclamation of Christ's new law of love, and to the

revelation of His love at the Last Supper. It looks forward to the full and social joy of the city of God in heaven, the joy of which the Eucharist is the anticipation and the pledge.

With the *First Sunday of the Passion,* we enter the second phase of the holy season. Now we are to go on from the contemplation of our sinfulness and weakness. We are to enter into the sufferings of Christ as He took on the full burden of our fallen human state, to bring it, in His loving obedience to His Father's will, through death to life.

As we pray the chants of the Passiontide and Holy Week Masses, we should remember that we are praying them *with Christ.* These songs of anguish and hope, these prayers for deliverance and help, were composed by one or another of God's servants in the Old Testament to express their own needs. But they were inspired by the Spirit so that Christ, *the* Holy Servant of God, might use them as His prayers when He took upon Himself all our human miseries. When we pray them, we express our own needs, true enough; but far more than this, we can pray them with Christ and with all His suffering members on earth. The Gospels give us very little of our Lord's thoughts and feelings as He went through His Passion. But these psalms used by the Church in her Passiontide liturgy give us the best way of entering into His sufferings, and of having in ourselves, as the Epistle for the Second Sunday of the Passion tells us, "that mind which was also in Christ Jesus."

These psalms also bring out the aspect of struggle, of mortal combat against fierce and powerful enemies, in the work of our redemption. This is the aspect also brought out by the Preface for this season: ". . . that whence death once issued, thence life should rise again; and he that once conquered by means of a tree, by a tree should be overcome." Our Lord is at once the "Lamb of God," going obediently to His sacrificial death, and the great Warrior against the enemies of God foreshadowed in His ancestor, King David.

On the First Sunday of the Passion, again, in the reading from the Epistle to the Hebrews, we listen to an explanation of the basic doctrine of Christ's death as the sacrifice of the New Covenant, by which we became heirs of eternal life. The Gospel begins the reading of St. John's Gospel, which continues during the following six days, describing the closing-in of the battle between our Lord and the powers of evil, during the last days of His earthly life.

The palm procession on the *Second Sunday of the Passion*—once *the* Sunday with this title—is a kind of prelude to the celebration of the paschal mysteries. The custom of renewing each year the joyful acclaim of the Hebrew crowds when our Lord rode in triumph into Jerusalem began, naturally enough, in Jerusalem itself, in the early centuries of the Church. The Jewish crowds had hailed our Lord as the promised Messiah, their Savior and King. How fitting, then, that we should do so each year before the celebration of the mysteries of our redemption, to show our faith in Him, our hope in His victory, our love. When we take part in the palm procession in our parish church, we should realize that by doing so we pledge our faith in Christ's redeeming work, our intention of going with Him through His Passion to the glory of His Resurrection—in the sacramental mysteries of Holy Week, and in our own lives.

The Mass itself of this Sunday is entirely devoted to the mystery of our redemption: the suffering and the glory, the passion and the resurrection. In the Collect prayer, the Gradual, and, above all, in Psalm 21 (Introit and Tract), the whole mystery is presented to us as a whole, so that we may try to understand it and enter into it more fully.

Almighty eternal God,
as you caused the Savior to take on our flesh
and to undergo the cross, so as
to give mankind an example of humility to imitate:
grant in your kindness,
that we may learn the lessons of his passion,
and share in his resurrection.

For study and discussion: In your Bible, see which psalms are quoted in the four accounts of the Passion. Read the whole of each. What other "scriptures" that were fulfilled by Christ's death and resurrection are given in the Masses of Passiontide? What graces does the Church want us to receive from taking part in her annual celebration of the mysteries of our redemption, as seen in the prayers of the Passiontide Masses?

CHAPTER 7   **THE**

PASCHAL

MYSTERY

W E ARE NOW APPROACHING the climax of the liturgical year, the celebration of the paschal mystery.
Theologically and historically, this is the first annual
celebration of the Church. It is the matrix of the
liturgical year—all other feasts celebrate one or other
aspect of the paschal mystery. All other feasts developed after this, the first and greatest.

We call this celebration "Holy Week," for it is
the most sacred week in the year. But when we do
so, we must be sure to include Easter itself in our
thinking. The better term is the name the Church
has always given it: *Pascha Domini*—the feast of the
Lord which is the fulfillment of the paschal celebration of Israel, the feast in which the true Paschal
Lamb is sacrificed for the salvation of the world.

Recent centuries tended to separate our Lord's
suffering and death from His glorification. But Holy
Scripture and the liturgy see them as one whole. St.

52

John speaks of Christ's "lifting up," of His "glorification" as one act including His passion, His death,
His resurrection and ascension (John 3:13-17; 7:39;
12:27-36). St. Paul tells us, in the Epistle used on
Easter Sunday, that "Christ our Pasch is sacrificed;
therefore let us feast."

At an earlier time, this unity was so well understood that the evening Mass on Holy Thursday
(marking the beginning of Good Friday), Good Friday itself, Holy Saturday and Easter Sunday were
all considered to be one feast, the celebration of the
Pascha Domini. Later generations did not understand this unity so clearly; our present Holy Week
includes the first three days of the week, and is too
often thought of as ending on Holy Saturday. But
the "renewal" of the Holy Week rites in 1956, by
returning the celebration of the Holy Night of the
Resurrection (the "Easter Vigil") to its proper place,
enables us once more to see and to enter into the
paschal mystery as a whole. The four first days of
Holy Week (Sunday through Wednesday) belong to
the Passiontide period of preparation; the paschal
celebration includes Holy Thursday, Good Friday,
and the Holy Night that culminates in the Mass for
Easter dawn.

When we begin to think of this celebration as
that of the "Pasch of the Lord," we begin to understand the mystery of our redemption in its historical
and social dimensions; we begin to see why it is the
central mystery of our Christian life. It was not by
chance that our Lord died at the time of the Jewish
Pasch or Passover. His death, as Scripture and

the liturgy indicate, was the fulfillment to which the Jewish Passover looked forward. Each year, at the Passover meal, through the centuries since the Exodus, the youngest child would ask his father: Why is this day different from all other days? And the father would once more recount God's wonderful deliverance of His people from their slavery in Egypt, during the night when the destroying angel passed over the houses marked with the blood of the Paschal Lamb, and when, with the Lord as their guide and protector, the Hebrews passed out of Egypt, through the Red Sea, to their new life as God's own and chosen people.

In God's design, the first Passover and its annual celebration took place in the springtime. It was a deliverance, and it was also a re-creation, making a holy people out of a mere multitude. And so this paschal celebration included all the resonances proper to celebrations of the annual re-creation of nature. (This is why a yearling *lamb,* born the previous spring, was eaten.) God's wonderful work of creating and renewing the world of nature each year was seen as the visible sign of His even more wonderful work of delivering and creating His people.

More than this, as the centuries of Jewish history went on, God's revelation increasingly focused their hopes on His promises for the future, for the times of the Messiah. All the wonderful deliverances throughout their history, especially the return from the Babylonian captivity and the victories of the Machabees, were seen as repetitions of the first great

deliverance of the Exodus, and also as preparations
and anticipations of the final deliverance to come.

Our Lord's redeeming death was the fulfillment
of this hope. The new Moses leads His People—all
redeemed mankind—out of slavery to Satan, destroying the power of sin and death, bringing His people
with Him to eternal life. This is the great deliverance, of which the great events of Jewish history
were preliminary stages. This is the new creation,
of which the creation of the world of nature and the
creation of God's people were preparations and fore-
shadowings.

Our paschal celebration is thus the fulfillment of
the Jewish Pasch. Christ is the true Paschal Lamb,
whose blood saves us from destruction. In this light
we see why the paschal celebration of the Church is
also the celebration of our baptism. For every baptism is a realization of Christ's redeeming work, delivering another human being from the power of the
Enemy, through the "Red Sea" of the baptismal
waters, to the life of God's holy people in the
Church.

At every Mass, as we know, the whole mystery of
Christ's redeeming death is re-presented. And in the
paschal celebration also the whole mystery is presented, from three viewpoints, as it were, in each of
the great days: Holy Thursday, Good Friday and the
Holy Night. These three viewpoints are all expressed in St. Paul's wonderful sentence used in
the Office for these days and also in the Gradual
on Holy Thursday. "For our sake, Christ became
obedient unto death—even the death of the Cross—

this is why God has exalted Him and given Him the Name that is above every name."

On Holy Thursday, the day of the Last Supper, we think especially of Our Lord's free offering of Himself, for love of us, in loving obedience to His Father's will. On Good Friday, we consider His redeeming death—the death of the cross. And during the Holy Night, we rejoice in His exaltation. Let us, then, now briefly consider the rites of the two first days, leaving those of the Holy Night to the following chapter.

On Holy Thursday, in former times, a bishop would sometimes celebrate as many as three Masses: one for the reconciliation of public penitents, one for the blessing and consecration of the Holy Oils, and the one of the "Supper of the Lord." Today, our bishop celebrates a special Chrism Mass in the morning, with the long and beautiful ceremonies of blessing the Oil of the catechumens and the Oil of the Sick, and of consecrating the Holy Chrism. And in our cathedral and in every parish church, the Mass *in coena Domini,* the Mass of the Last Supper, is celebrated in the late afternoon or evening. (The Collect, which might not seem to rhyme with the rest of the Proper, was actually taken from the Mass of Wednesday in Holy Week).

In this Mass of the Supper, we see the mystery of Christ's redeeming death in the light of love: the Father's love of us, Christ's love of His Father which made Him obedient even to death; His love for us which caused Him to lay down His life for His friends and to leave us the Eucharist, the sacrifice and sacrament of love. By instituting the Eucharist, the sacrifice of the New Covenant, our Lord committed Himself, freely gave Himself up to His coming death, already sacramentally present and anticipated in His Eucharist.

Even if it is not possible to hold the ceremony of the Washing of the Feet at this Mass in our parish church, we can use the prayers of this rite for our meditations on this holy day: "A new command I give you, that you love one another as I have loved you, said the Lord. . . . Where charity and love abide, there is God. . . . The love of Christ has gathered us together, let us rejoice and be glad in him." Most of us will not have the opportunity to lay down our lives for love of others in one heroic act. But all of us can do this day by day, by "washing one another's feet," that is, serving one another in whatever ways we can, however humble these ways may be: "An example I have given you, that you may do likewise."

The ceremonies of Good Friday consist of various parts which, in the course of time, were combined into one single service. In the first part, the Readings and the Prayers, we pray as the Church prayed many centuries ago, before much of the modern development of the liturgy. There is no "entrance rite"; the celebrant comes in, prays, and we all sit down to listen to readings from the Old Testament and the New, with appropriate chants in between. These readings of the prophecies and the historical reality of Christ's Passion, are followed by the "Prayers of the Faithful," the solemn prayers of intercession for all classes in the Church and for all

mankind, which were once part of every "synaxis."
It is, perhaps, peculiarly appropriate that these
prayers should be retained in the Good Friday service, to remind us that Christ died for all mankind.

The Adoration of the Cross which follows is of
later origin—like the Palm Procession, borrowed
from the liturgy of Jerusalem, introduced into
Rome when a relic of the true cross was brought
there, and later spreading to all Western churches.
We need to realize that the "Reproaches" sung
while we are going up to kiss the crucifix are not
directed at God's people of old so much as at *us,*
His new people, here and now. We have been delivered from slavery to the devil; we have been led
and guided by Christ's light, fed and given drink
by the Eucharist; given a share in Christ's royal
dignity and the glory of everlasting life. Yet whenever we have sinned, whenever we have injured
any of Christ's brethren, we have rejected Christ
and crucified Him.

The last part of the Good Friday rites is the Communion Service. It may still seem strange to some of
us to be allowed to receive Communion on this day,
after so many years when we could not. Yet the
restoration of Good Friday Communion in 1956
gave back to us the traditional practice of the
Church. There was never any celebration of the
Eucharistic Sacrifice on this day, but priests and
people alike received Communion (in fact, during
the Middle Ages, many people made their Easter
Communion, their "Easter duty" as we call it, on
Good Friday). This is, obviously, the day above all

others on which to "proclaim the death of the Lord," as we do whenever we eat this bread (1 Cor. 11).

For study and discussion: Read the Chrism Mass. What do the blessings of the Oils and the consecration of the Chrism teach us about the sacraments in which these are used? What does the Gospel for Holy Thursday teach us about taking part in this Mass? In any Mass? How do the psalms used at the Mandatum bring out the wonder of our Lord's doing what He did? Why does the Church want us to take part in the Mass of Holy Thursday and the solemn Good Friday service in preference to any other devotions on these days?

CHAPTER 8 **THE HOLY PASCHAL NIGHT**

THE CEREMONIES OF THIS HOLY NIGHT make up the greatest, the most vital celebration in the whole liturgical year. The name, Easter Vigil, now given to it perhaps conceals its true nature and function from us, rather than helping us to understand it. It is, indeed, the "mother of all vigils," the original night watch of the Church for the dawn of the day of the Lord's Resurrection, culminating in the Holy Sacrifice which makes Him present in our midst. In all vigils, the Church, the Bride, watches and prays in expectation of the return of the Bridegroom. And this Easter night watch is the vigil *par excellence.*

But the word no longer brings to our minds the idea of watching and praying through the *night* in expectation and preparation for some glorious event. It makes us think rather of the *day* before a great feast, the "vigil of Christmas," for instance. The reason is that all the Church's vigils were once, on the

60

pattern of this greatest one, the paschal vigil, night-watches for the return of the Savior. But gradually, for various reasons including a decline in appreciation of their meaning, such services were transferred to the morning of the previous day. The Mass that was designed to be the climax of the vigil at dawn, the first celebration of the feast, was also transferred to the previous morning.

This change of time may not matter so much with the Vigil of Christmas, for instance, or with those of the Ember Saturdays. But it entirely obscured the meaning of this great night-watch for the Resurrection. In 1956, it was once more restored to its rightful place in time. It will take some years certainly before it is restored to its rightful place in our understanding and appreciation, before we realize fully that this is *the* Easter service, the paschal celebration, with all that this implies.[2] Let us, then, study the structure and the themes of the ceremonies of this Holy Night, so that we may begin to understand better why it is the chief celebration of the whole Christian year.

We should keep in mind, throughout, all the meanings of "the Pasch of the Lord" indicated in the previous chapter. In this Holy Night, we celebrate the mystery of our Redeemer, of how His humiliation proved to be the cause of His ultimate glory at the right hand of the Father. This glory was revealed to the world by the angel sitting beside the empty tomb, and by the women who were the first to announce the gospel of Jesus' victory, which is at the same time the gospel of man's redemption. For in Him our human nature arose from death, the effect and penalty of sin, to the radiant life of a humanity completely possessed and transfigured by the Spirit of God, a life wholly charged with the Spirit, wholly "lived to God," triumphant and glorious.

And in this Holy Night, Christ, the new Moses, leads us with Him from slavery to freedom, from death to life. Those who are baptized on this night are brought by His power through the Red Sea of the baptismal water. Plunged in His death, as St. Paul says, they are re-born of the Spirit to the life of Christ, eternal life. Clothed in radiant white, they take part for the first time in offering Christ's sacrifice and take part in the Eucharistic Banquet, the bread given them by their heavenly Father, the sign and foretaste of the banquet of heaven. And we who are already baptized are renewed in the grace of our baptism, by the ceremonies of this Holy Night and our renewed faith, and are caught up anew in the great current of Christ's rising from the dead to His glorious life in the Father's presence.

The first rite of this Holy Night is the celebration of the light of Christ. All the meanings of light in the feasts of Christmas and Epiphany are gathered up here and given new force. The light of Christ has not only come down into our dark world, but it has descended into the far deeper darkness of the world of the dead to break open the prison-house and bring the captives of Satan up to the light of eternal life. As, in the first Passover night, the Lord led His people out of Egypt by the pillar of fiery light, so now the light of Christ, shining out to our eyes in the light of the Paschal candle, leads us to life of the heavenly kingdom. As the flame of the Paschal

candle spreads out to the candles of Christ's ministers and then to our own, so we are caught up by
baptism into the radiance of Christ's own light; we
are to radiate it to the dark world, as we await in
hope our final crossing-over into the glory of the
Lord, into the world of the Resurrection.

This ceremony of the lighting of the paschal
candle serves as the introduction to the nucleus of
the whole service—in the traditional vigil form—in
which God speaks to us in the readings from Holy
Scripture, and we respond to His word by chants
and prayers. These readings, chants and prayers
make us at once understand and celebrate the full
meaning of this Holy Night.

The first reading, the story of the first creation,
with the prayer that follows, leads us into the mystery of the redemption as the new creation, far more
wonderful than the first. The second reading shows
us the mystery of our redemption as the new Pasch,
giving us the description of the Exodus, the Hebrew
people going out of Egypt through the Red Sea and
the destruction of their enemies in the water. The
chant that follows offers our response of praise; and
the prayer asks God, who is now renewing this wonderful work of His power in our midst by the sacrament of baptism, to bring all mankind to share in
the inheritance of the new Israel of the Spirit.

The third reading, from Isaias, and the chant and
the prayer, lead us into the mystery of the Church,
the home of God's glory, the vine which is Christ,
and asks the grace that we, His members, may bring
forth good fruit.

And the fourth reading, with its chant, gives us

Moses' warning to the Hebrew people of old that we must be faithful to the grace of our deliverance, of our baptism. The following prayer humbly asks for the grace to do so.

At the beginning of the third part, the blessing of the baptismal water, we all join in the litany and, by invoking the Saints, ask the prayers of the whole Church triumphant. Then the celebrant prepares the water for baptism, accompanying his actions of exorcism and blessing with a long and beautiful prayer.

The theme of this blessing is what God has done with this creature of His, water, in the Old Testament, using it, in accordance with its nature, as a means of destruction—in the Flood and in the Red Sea—and as a principle of life—in creation, in the garden of Paradise, in the Flood, in the desert. This same theme is carried on into the New Testament by what Christ did with water during His earthly life: changing it into wine, walking on it, being baptized in it, causing it to pour forth from His side on the cross, commanding His apostles to baptize all nations in it. All these are promises of what God does by means of water in baptism. The celebrant prays that God will now fulfill these promises, and give this water the power of God to wash away sin, to destroy the old life of fallen human nature, and bring forth a new race, re-born of the Spirit.

Throughout this prayer, we should notice the repeated mention and invocation of the Holy Spirit. We are reborn to eternal life of water and the Spirit. As the Spirit hovered over the primeval waters to make them fruitful for the first creation, so, the celebrant prays that the power of the Spirit may come down into this water, to make it fruitful for the new creation, the birth of children of God.

And all the spiritual meanings that Scripture and the liturgy attach to oil, which heals and strengthens, makes supple and beautiful, and the meaning of the Chrism (oil and sweet-smelling herbs), which is the sign of our receiving the Spirit as the principle of our new life, are brought in also when the celebrant pours into the baptismal water, first the baptismal "Oil of Catechumens," and finally the holy Chrism.

Then the sacrament of baptism is administered to those who have been preparing for it during the past weeks. And we, who have been preparing for the renewal of the grace of our baptism by our lenten efforts, renew our baptismal "promises," that is, our solemn self-commitment to renounce Satan and to serve Christ our Redeemer faithfully in His Church. We seal our renewed commitment by reciting together the great baptismal prayer of the baptized, of those who have been reborn as "sons in the Son" —the Our Father. And we are sprinkled with the blessed water, set aside for this purpose, as the sign of our inward renewal. We then join in the second half of the litany, imploring the aid of our Savior by reminding Him of all He did and suffered for our sake, to give us and all mankind all needed blessings.

Newly dead to sin, newly risen with Christ, we are now ready to take part with the Church in His sacrifice of praise, as we had never taken part in the Mass before. The liturgy of this Mass, the first Mass of the Feast of the Resurrection, is very ancient (there is no Introit, no Credo, no "Last Gospel"). In the Epistle, St. Paul tells us "you are risen with Christ." We are to seek the good things that are on high, where Christ is, seated at the right hand of God. For "you are dead"—to the life of slavery to sin from which Christ has freed us—and "your life is hidden with Christ in God. Christ is your life; when He appears on the great day (of Judgment), then you too will appear with Him in glory."

The Alleluia—the word in which the Church sums up her Easter joy—is solemnly intoned by the celebrant and echoed by the whole congregation, before the Gospel announces to us the mystery of the empty tomb: "He is risen, He is not here."

Joy in Christ's victory, joy in our new life in God, prayer for the love of one another in the Church which is the gift of the Spirit of adoption, prayer to attain, through celebrating this feast on earth, to the eternal paschal celebration of heaven—these are the themes of this Mass of Easter dawn, which concludes with the dawn praise of Christ's light, the prayer of Lauds.

For study and discussion: Look up the texts in Scripture of the various references given in the *Exsultet* and in the blessing of the baptismal water. What could be done in your family, your parish, to make people more aware of the importance of the service of the Holy Night, and to help them take part more appreciatively and fruitfully?

NOTES

1 Holy Saturday itself is once again "a-liturgical"—that is, having no liturgical celebration proper to it—the ceremonies of the Holy Night being properly the opening of the Easter celebration. Holy Saturday is the time for our material preparations for the Easter celebration, and for thinking particularly about the mystery of our Lord's "descent into hell," that is, into the very realm of the dead. Recent piety has almost ignored this aspect of our Lord's redeeming work, although it is one which in early English literature, for example, was a favorite theme—the "harrowing of hell": our Lord as the young Hero bringing light into the dark prison-house of "the world below," breaking the bolts and chains of death, to bring the souls of the just with Him up to eternal life and light.

2 Many pious people who go to daily Mass throughout the year still feel that they are "missing something" when the celebration of the Holy Night is placed, as it should be, so that at least the Mass comes after midnight, and they cannot receive Holy Communion both on Holy Saturday and on Easter Sunday. But when we understand the special and vital importance of the Holy Night as *the* Easter celebration of the whole Church, and the significance of our participation in the Mass that is its culmination, the question of the number of opportunities to communicate is seen in proper proportion.

On the other hand, it seems very sad that so many people who have spent Lent making so many efforts at prayer and self-sacrifice, are still willing to miss the "Easter Vigil"—the great service and act of the Church toward which all our lenten penance is ordered. We have tried all during Lent to prepare ourselves for this renewal of the grace of baptism. How can we bear to miss taking part in this renewal if it is in any way possible? (Many of the same people would not miss the Christmas Midnight Mass for anything.) To wait to come to church until it is time for the Mass itself to begin, shows a complete lack of understanding of the meaning of the Holy Night. It is by taking part, in faith and hope and love, in all that leads up to the Mass that we make ready to live a new paschal life (the life whose central act is participation in the Holy Sacrifice), and to share in the joy of Christ and His Church.

CHAPTER 9 **THE EASTER OCTAVE AND THE SUNDAYS AFTER EASTER**

IN THE LATIN CHURCH, the keynote of the Easter season has become the one word: Alleluia.[1] In it the Church sums up everything she wants to say to God —praise, thanksgiving—and in it she expresses her own overflowing joy. The Church sings this holy word over and over again during the paschal season, and wants us all to sing it with her: "Praise, shout with joy to the Lord." [2]

During the eight days of the Easter octave, the Church is celebrating in a special way her joy in the victory of Christ and our victory in Him. In the Epistles of this week, we hear the primitive proclamation of the faith, the first sermons of the apostles after Pentecost. Jesus who died on the cross, God has raised from the dead and established as Judge of the living and the dead, who will absolve from their sins all those who believe in Him. In raising Him from the dead, God has fulfilled all the promises of the

Old Testament. In His human nature, Jesus is now *the Lord,* risen and glorious at the right hand of the Father, the conqueror of sin and death. The Gospels of these eight days also proclaim the fact of the Resurrection, through the accounts of our Lord's appearances to His own: the apostles are allowed to touch Jesus' glorified body. And our Lord Himself declares His rising from the dead: "It was fitting that Christ should suffer and so enter into his glory."

In every Mass this week, Psalm 117 is used. It is the song of the Victor whom God has enabled to triumph over his enemies and who is now entering into the presence of God in His temple while His people acclaim Him with joy. "This is the day the Lord has made, let us be glad and rejoice in it." The Easter octave makes up one great day of rejoicing, a foretaste of eternal happiness. Psalm 104 is also used more than once. It is a psalm celebrating the wonderful work of the Exodus, the first Passover, for Easter celebrates Christ's leading us with Him through death to life, from slavery into freedom as God's people. And the other psalms used are, similarly, praises of God's redeeming power, joy in His wonderful works in our behalf.

The Introit refrains of the Masses from Easter Monday through Low Sunday praise God for the blessings He gives us as His people—here and now in the sacraments, and visibly and in perfect fullness in heaven. This is how we are to understand the references to Israel's liberation which we find in the liturgy. The Church is the "land flowing with milk and honey," with the food and drink of God's Word and the Eucharist. Here we are given the "water of wisdom." The water of baptism is the sign and fig-ure of the life-giving Spirit of truth and life that flows through the Church and all her members. At our baptism, and our Easter renewal of it, Christ says to each of us: "Come, blessed of my Father, re-ceive the kingdom. . . ." The Church is the king-dom, in pledge and preparation and anticipation. By baptism, our mouths were opened to make us able to proclaim the praises of God, to pray to Him as our Father. By baptism, our enemies were de-stroyed, and we, the chosen of God, were led out of slavery, with rejoicing. And the prayers of the Masses ask for the graces we need worthily to live the life given us at baptism so as to receive its full-ness in eternity.

During this Easter week, then, we are to live in the newness and joy of the life given us at baptism, the paschal joy of the redeemed. In the early Church, the newly baptized wore all week the white garment given them at baptism, and met each day to hear an instruction on the sacraments and to take part in the Mass. Before their baptism and confirmation, first Mass and Holy Communion—all during the Holy Night—they had not been clearly told how the Lord would have them partake of His bounty in the Church. Only after they had actually been admitted into the Church and received the holy gift, was the doctrine on the sacrament and the sacrifice ex-plained. During this week, then, we are given the graces of a new joy and new appreciation of our life in Christ, of what it means to be redeemed and to be members of God's holy people.

The Sundays after Easter [2] continue the same themes, developing them from various aspects. The Mass of the Second Sunday is built around the image of the Good Shepherd. He who was called "the Shepherd of Israel" in the Old Testament has revealed Himself in Jesus, the Good Shepherd who gives His life for His sheep. We, His flock, are to gather round Him in joy, to follow His example, to receive His mysteries in the Church so as to be transformed into His likeness.

The Mass of the Third Sunday shows us the unfailing source of the joy that should be ours, even here on earth where we are "strangers and pilgrims" (Epistle). In the Gospel, taken from our Lord's discourse at the Last Supper, He tells His apostles "A little while and you shall not see me, and again a little while and you shall see me . . . your sorrow will be turned into joy, a joy no man can take from you." The "little while" was the three days of His Passion. When He rose from the dead, and the disciples saw Him again, their sorrow was turned into joy. And their joy was not taken from them when He ascended into heaven, for He is still invisibly present in His Church, present among us whenever we gather together in His Name and take part in His Eucharist. This is our primal Christian joy: joy in the presence of Christ risen and glorious, joy that, as His members, we are in the Father's presence with Him. This is the joy that no one can take from us, the joy that should make our Christian life radiant with happiness even in cares and troubles, so that, as the Epistle tells us, everyone who sees how we act

will be led thereby to give glory to God and to want
to share our gladness. But since our present joy
comes from seeing Christ by faith, and not yet in
open vision, we can also understand this "little
while" as being all the centuries between Christ's
ascension and His return in glory; we can understand it of our Christian life on earth. For all this
time that seems so long to us is really only "a little
while" in comparison with the eternal life that will
be ours in secure possession and unfailing joy in the
world to come.

The Mass of the Fourth Sunday begins to show us
how we are thus taken up into the very life of God,
even here on earth. In the Gospel, again from the
discourse at the Last Supper, our Lord tells us the
reason for His great journey through death back to
the Father who sent Him. "It is for your good that
I am going. If I did not go, the Spirit would not
come to you. But if I go, I will send him to you."
The Holy Spirit will guide the apostles toward the
fullness of truth. He will show the world what sin is
—to refuse to believe in Christ; what holiness is—to
share in Christ's life with His Father; what the judgment is—Satan and all who finally refuse God are
already judged. The Spirit will show Christ's glory,
for it is His truth that He will proclaim.

The prayer over the offerings of this Mass asks:
"O God, as by the holy exchanges of this sacrifice,
you make us partakers of the divine life; grant, we
ask, that as we know thy truth, we may put it into
practice by fitting ways of life and action." It is because we received the gift of the Holy Spirit in bap-

tism and confirmation that we can take part in the
"holy exchanges" of the Mass. Sharing in the Spirit
of Christ, we can take part in His act of praise and
love, offering ourselves with Christ in the Spirit to
the Father. And when we take part in the Mass and
receive the Body of Christ, we receive a fuller in-
flowing of this Spirit, in which we are united to the
Father as "sons in the Son."

The Mass of the Fifth Sunday shows us the conse-
quence of this wonderful sharing in the very life of
God. "If you ask the Father anything in my Name,
he will give it to you—ask and you shall receive that
your joy may be full. . . . For the Father himself
loves you, because you love me and believe that I
have come from God." In his sermon on this Gospel,
read in the Breviary this Sunday, St. Augustine explains what it means to "ask in the Name of Christ":
to ask what is for our salvation, what is for our true
joy. If we ask for anything that the Father sees would
interfere with this, then He will give us something
else instead, something that will lead us to fuller life
and joy.

Psalm 65 is used on all these last three Sundays.
This is another paschal song, praising God for redeeming us through suffering. "Come, see the works
of God: . . . He has given life to our souls, not allowed our feet to stumble. . . . You have tried us, O
God, we have gone through fire and water, then you
led us out to freedom." Let us pray all the psalms
used in these Masses of Easter week and the Easter
season, especially 117 and this one, 65, as our paschal
prayers. And let us try to live in the spirit of these

psalms, the spirit of Christian joy: "Come and hear, all you who fear God, what great things he has done for my soul!" [3]

For study and discussion: Take the Introits of the Masses of Easter week and recite them, repeating the refrain (the first text given in the Missal) between each verse of the whole psalm. What insight does this give us into what God does for us in the Church? Read the entire chapters in the Acts from which the Epistles of Easter Monday, Tuesday and Wednesday are taken. What could be done in your family, your parish, to make the paschal season as much of a reality in people's lives as Lent and Holy Week?

NOTES

1 *Hallelu* in Hebrew means to praise, sing, shout with joy. *Ja* is the abbreviation of the sacred Name: Yahweh—the name which God revealed to Moses—not a generic term like "god" in English, but His "personal" Name, which, scholars tell us, means "I am who I am." Halleluja, or in its Greek and Latinized form, Alleluia, thus sums up all praise of the creating, revealing and redeeming God. It is no vague expression of general happiness; it is at once a shout, a song, a prayer to the God who reveals Himself to us in Christ in the Spirit. And so St. John and the Fathers say that Alleluia is the essence of the "new song" of the redeemed, which we are rehearsing here on earth to sing in full joy in heaven.

2 The paschal season is, properly, fifty days long—seven full weeks plus the crowning and completing day of Pentecost. The Church sees this as one great "day" celebrating the paschal mystery—prefigured in the Old Law by the period from the feast of the Passover to that of the giving of the law on Mt. Sinai—and we might note that it is actually longer than the forty-day preparatory period of Lent.

3   So many Catholics observe the holy season of Lent, but how few the holy season of Easter. So many go to Mass every day during Lent, so few even during the Easter octave. Surely, having made the preparation, we should join in the celebration. Surely when we have tried to share our Lord's sufferings, He would like us to share in His joy.

CHAPTER 10 **THE FEAST**

OF

THE ASCENSION

AFTER THE CONSECRATION in every Mass, we commemorate the Ascension of our Lord into glory: ". . . we thy servants and also thy holy people, in memory of the most blessed passion and the resurrection from the dead and also the ascension into glory of Christ, thy Son, our Lord. . . ." We should not understand this to mean that the Ascension is something new and distinct, but rather that it is another aspect of the one paschal mystery. Originally, there was no separate celebration of the Ascension; it became a special feast not simply because the Church wanted to follow the chronological order of events, but rather because the Easter mystery is so rich that it is impossible to give all its aspects due emphasis in one single celebration.

At Easter, we celebrate especially Christ's victory over death, our real life, Christ the giver of that life. On Ascension day, we celebrate the effect of Christ's victory: now the barrier between earth and heaven is taken away. In the glorified Lord, mankind enters into heaven; man redeemed has in Christ, as it were, a right to heaven: our Brother, our Head is already there. As the special *Communicantes* of the feast says: "on this day he established in the Father's glory the substance of our weak humanity which he had united with himself." And the Preface for the feast tells us why: "that he might make us partakers in his divinity."

There are two themes, then, in this feast: the glorification of the manhood of Christ, above every creature, "at the right hand" of the Father, that is, sharing in His royal power as King and Judge; and our glorification in Him. It is our own weak human nature ("like us in all things save sin") that is thus transfigured, charged with the glory of God, exalted at the Father's right hand. Christ took on this human nature and brought it through death to this glory so that we might ascend with Him and in Him. Our glorified Lord is "the final man," the true exemplar of what men henceforth are to aspire to, and are enabled to approach by His grace.

The first theme is brought out in the Gospel, and also in all the chants of the Mass, using Psalm 46 and Psalm 67. Psalm 46 is a song celebrating the final victory of God and the establishment of His kingdom. Containing the lines: "God goes up to his throne amid shouts of joy, the Lord, with the sound of the trumpet," it has been used by the Church from early times to praise Christ triumphantly returning to His Father's glory. Psalm 76 is a song of victory describing the whole history of Israel as one great triumphant march of the Lord with His people, from Egypt to His temple on Mt. Sion. So Christ leads redeemed mankind, overthrowing their enemies, establishing His kingdom, up to the heavenly sanctuary.

The second theme is brought out in the Preface and in the three prayers of the Mass, especially the Collect. "Grant, we pray, O almighty God, that, as we believe that your Son, our Redeemer, today ascended into heaven, so may we also dwell in spirit in the heavens." As St. Leo says so beautifully in the Breviary lesson of this feast: "Christ's ascension is our uplifting; and whither our Head has gone before us in glory, there also are we called in hope. Let us, then, dearest brethren, rejoice with fitting gladness, and be happy, giving thanks. For today we were not only confirmed in the possession of paradise; in Christ we have gone into the height of heaven; we have gained more through the unutterable kindness of Christ than we lost through the envy of the devil."

This feast, then, like that of the Assumption which is its complement, is a great feast of Christian hope, and of joy in that hope. Here we find the principle of an essentially Christian "humanism," of the Christian teaching about the value of man, the whole man, soul and body. Here and now, though we cannot experience it, we share in Christ's heavenly glory as His members—heaven really is our destination, and in Christ we have already arrived at our goal. Where He is, there we shall also be some day, body and soul, by His grace.

But there is one more theme in the Mass of this

feast—the theme of the Christian life here and now, as it is to be lived between the visible return of the Lord to heaven and His coming again. The Introit gives this theme as the keynote to the whole feast, and it is taken from the Epistle which recounts the historical fact of the Ascension, repeating the angel's words to the apostles: "Men of Galilee, why are you standing lost in wonder, looking up to heaven. He whom you have seen going up into heaven, shall return in the same way."

Our Christian life is not meant to be spent in standing around, wistfully looking toward the Lord we cannot see. He is enthroned at the right hand of the Father as our High Priest and King, "living always to make intercession for us," to communicate His life and grace to men, to bring us with Him to the Father.

Before He withdrew His visible presence, He had told His apostles what to do: return to Jerusalem for the fulfillment of the promise of the Father, and then to be Christ's witnesses to the uttermost parts of the earth, making disciples of all nations, baptizing them and teaching them Christ. And we have the same commission today, according to our vocation. We have to help prepare for the Lord's return, to witness to Him, to bring all men to Him, to share our life and our hope. This is the right way of longing for His second coming. But we can only do this if we too are "charged with power from on high."

So the Feast of the Ascension looks forward to the "completing" Feast of Pentecost, the outpouring of the Spirit. The days between the Ascension and Pentecost form the great and the original "Novena," nine days' prayer. Whatever other novenas we take part in during the year, we should certainly make this one. As the apostles obeyed Christ's final command and returned to Jerusalem to the "upper room" where they "with one mind continued steadfastly in prayer, together with the women and Mary, the mother of Jesus, and with his brethren," so during these days the whole Church is praying for a fuller outpouring of the Spirit which Christ sent from the Father on the first Pentecost.

It would be entirely wrong to interpret the Ascension as something sad, as a departure. Neither the apostles nor we have been left orphaned. The mystery of Pentecost will give the full revelation of how close the Lord is to us. The Vespers of the Feast of the Ascension gives us a wonderful prayer to use during these nine days of prayer preparing for Pentecost.

O King of glory, Lord of might,
who today ascended as victor above the heavens,
leave us not orphaned,
but send us the promise of the Father,
the Spirit of truth, alleluia.

For study and discussion: How might an appreciation of the mystery of the Ascension change the quality of much of our prayer, of our attitude to religion, to life? What could be done in homes and parishes to foster participation in the great novena of the Church?

NOTE

1 Many people today feel a conflict between the idea of Christ going up into heaven, and our modern knowledge

of the solar system, "space," etc. It should be pointed out that the conflict is only in the realm of images, not reality. Nobody knows the relationship of a glorified body to space; by His Resurrection to the state of glory, our Lord's humanity became superior to physical conditions of time and space. His visible Ascension was the external manifestation of His rising above the limitations of human nature as we know it, and becoming transformed into glorious human nature, wholly permeated with the Spirit of power and freedom and love. Whether such a human nature needs a "where" in our sense is something God has not told us. In any case, it is not a "place" to be found by explorations of "space." But we need some picture of "where" our Lord ascended and His Mother was assumed, and "up" has always been the direction mankind has considered the region of life and light.

CHAPTER 11

THE FEAST
OF PENTECOST
AND ITS OCTAVE,
TRINITY SUNDAY

THE GREAT FEAST of Pentecost is the completion of the paschal celebration. The word simply means the "fiftieth" day after Easter. But it was fifty days after delivering the Israelites from Egypt by opening up the Red Sea and destroying their enemies that God appeared to them in the fiery cloud covering Mt. Sinai, gave them His law and made His covenant with them, establishing them as His holy people. It was also on the fiftieth day after His redeeming us by His death and resurrection that Christ sent down on the apostles, gathered in the Upper Room, the "promise of the Father," the Holy Spirit, in wind and fire, engraving His law of love in their hearts, and proclaiming them as the New Israel to which henceforth all men are called to belong.

During the centuries of Jewish history, God's holy men and His prophets saw more and more clearly how unfaithful His people were to His law, how, apparently, they simply could not be true to Him, the living God, nor be just and merciful to one another. They saw that what was needed was not so much deliverance from the tyranny of other nations, nor even from tyrants within Israel, as deliverance from sin and an entirely new beginning. And God, in answer, promised that He would do more than even the best and wisest of men would think possible. He would not only cleanse them from their sins, but would send His Spirit to give them a new spirit and a new heart to love Him and one another. He would send His Spirit to re-create His people so that they could offer Him worship "in Spirit and in Truth" and obey His law of justice and love.

This outpouring of God's Spirit was promised for the times of the Messiah, the Redeemer and King to come. The Spirit is mentioned at the Annunciation, and many times throughout the Gospels. Especially in the Gospel of St. John does our Lord speak of the Spirit, and most of all in His discourse at the Last Supper, one passage of which is used as the Gospel for Pentecost.

This, then, is the great promise, made by God in the Old Testament and renewed and deepened by Christ both before and after His Resurrection, which was fulfilled on the first Pentecost. Then, as the Preface for the feast sings, Christ, having ascended into heaven and taken His royal throne at the right hand of the Father, poured out the promised Spirit on the adopted children of God. And this same promise is daily being fulfilled in our midst whenever anyone is baptized, confirmed, ordained, receives the grace of any sacrament, grows in grace

in any way. For all this is the work of the Spirit in
the Church.

The first theme of the liturgy of Pentecost is praise
of this marvelous outflowing, abundant, "impetu-
ous" generosity of God to all men: His love which
is His Spirit, symbolized in rushing wind and
tongues of fire. "The Spirit of the Lord has filled the
whole world" sings the Introit. "I will pour out my
Spirit on all mankind," says the prophecy given in
one of the Lessons of Pentecost Saturday and quoted
by St. Peter in Wednesday's Epistle. Each day of the
octave, the Church repeats (from Psalm 103, praising the creating and re-creating Spirit of God):
"Send forth your Spirit and all things shall be
created, and you will renew the face of the earth."
The Preface of each day says that the whole earth is
overflowing with this joy of the Spirit and exults together with the angels.

The Spirit breaks all the bounds and limits of
the Old Dispensation. The cleansing and new life of
the Spirit, fruit of Christ's redeeming work, is for
all mankind. The new Israel is "of the Spirit" and
knows no limits of race or speech. In the Epistle, we
see the apostles proclaiming the wonderful works of
God so that men of all nations and tongues could
hear them "each in the language in which he was
born."

The mystery of the Church is thus also a theme of
the Pentecost liturgy. The mystery of the Spirit and
that of the Church are so inseparable that the Creed
has us profess our belief in both in the same breath:

"I believe in the Holy Ghost, the holy Catholic Church." "It seems good to the Holy Spirit and to us," announced the first Council of the Apostles. "The Spirit and the Bride say 'Come' " to the Lord Jesus all through the centuries until His return, the Apocalypse tells us. For Christ has given the Spirit to His Bride to be her Spirit. It is in the Church, the Mystical Body of Christ, that we receive and live by the Spirit.

Because He is the inner principle of the life of the Church, He is also working in all those who are living with Christ, who truly belong to the Church. The beautiful Sequence of Pentecost as well as the prayers of these Masses bring out all the wonderful things He will do for everyone of us, if we allow Him to work in us—cleansing, straightening out, warming, refreshing, making supple and fruitful. What He does is all summed up in St. Paul's phrase used in the Epistle for Pentecost Saturday: "The love of God is poured forth in our hearts by the Holy Spirit who has been given to us."

A final theme of Pentecost is the full revelation of the Blessed Trinity, of the intimate relations between God and the Church and therefore with every one of us individually. For the mystery of the Spirit and the Church leads us to the mystery of the Blessed Trinity, celebrated in a special way on the first Sunday after Pentecost. The celebration of the Blessed Trinity is, of course, always central to the liturgy, and so there is no special "devotion" directed toward the Blessed Trinity. But this feast is meant to remind us of this central place of the Trin-

ity in all Christian devotion, which we come to understand from the various aspects of the paschal
mystery.

The Son was sent into the world to bring all who
believe in Him back with Him to the Father, in the
Spirit. By baptism, we are re-born of water and the
Spirit, re-born as "sons in the Son." "And because
you are sons, God has sent the Spirit of His Son into
our hearts, crying 'Abba, Father.'" The Spirit who
is given to us "gives testimony to our spirit that we
are sons of God." The Spirit "prays within us" to
the Father, since we cannot pray rightly by ourselves.

Thus the whole purpose of our Lord's redeeming
work is to introduce us into His very life as the Son
of the Father, life in the Spirit who is love in person.
Our Lord tells us in the Gospel for Pentecost Sunday
that if we obey His word—that is, His command of
love for one another—then the Father will love us,
and He and the Father will come and dwell in us
and communicate Their Spirit. In the community
of love which is the Church, we are drawn into the
very life of overflowing love which is the life of the
Son with His Father, the mystery of the innermost
life of God.

The mystery [1] of the most Holy Trinity, therefore, was not revealed to us to be the "supreme test
of faith," as it is often, unfortunately, presented. It
is the secret of God's inner life, revealed to us because we are called to enter into it through Christ in
the Spirit, in the Church which is Christ's body. It
is almost an insult to the Father's wonderful love,
coming to gather us up through His Son into this
very current of the divine life, to speak about the

doctrine of the Blessed Trinity as an abstract theological puzzle. For it is the ultimate reality of our life in Christ.[2]

Let us, then, during the Pentecost octave,[3] ask the Holy Spirit to come with His sevenfold gift, giving witness to our spirit that we are truly the children of God—"and if sons, heirs also, co-heirs with Christ" —binding us together in the peace and love of Christ.

For study and discussion: Look through the Gospel of St. John, noting all the references to the Holy Spirit. How do these references help us to appreciate what He does in the Church? In each of us? The Acts of the Apostles have been called the "Gospel of the Spirit." Read some of the first chapters and see why. Make a list of the graces of the Spirit asked for in the Pentecost liturgy. Does this help to make His work in the Church and in us seem more real and vital?

NOTES

1   A great deal of research has been done in recent decades on the meaning of the word "mystery" as used by St. Paul, the liturgy, and early Christian tradition. The result has been to bring out the fact that the word does *not* mean primarily "something we cannot understand," but rather something sacred, hidden in the wisdom of God, which, it is true, human wisdom cannot attain to, but which God in His love reveals to us, above all, in His incarnate Son. Thus the "mystery of Christ" is the whole wonderful design of God's love for our salvation through the life, death and resurrection of His incarnate Son, revealed and realized in Christ, through the Church. When we speak of the "mystery of the Trinity," we mean: "what the Father has revealed to us through Christ of the inner life of the Godhead in which we are called to share through His Son in the Spirit."

2 As St. Hilary says in his treatise on the Blessed Trinity: heretics force us to formulate what cannot be expressed by means of human words . . . whereas we ought to be content to find, by a simple faith, what we have to do, namely: to adore the Father, to honor the Son together with Him, and to be filled with the Holy Spirit (II, 2).

3 The octave of Pentecost was added on to the Pentecost celebration at a time when people were not very clearly aware of the meaning of the "fiftieth day" as the completion and fulfillment of the whole paschal mystery. But the Masses for these days give us many insights into the mystery of Pentecost.

CHAPTER 12   THE SUNDAYS
               AFTER
               PENTECOST

THIS SEASON "after Pentecost" is the long summer
and fall of the liturgical year. The life given us at
baptism, renewed by the paschal celebration in the
springtime, is now given a time to ripen and bear
fruit. The general theme of these Sundays is, then,
our Christian life itself, in the tension of our present
state *"in via,"* on the way toward the life of the
world to come. The joy of Christ's victory, the joy of
our redemption renewed in the paschal season,
echoes in all these Masses. We truly do share His life
in faith and hope and love. In the Mass, "the whole
work of our redemption is renewed." Each Sunday's
Mass, then, is a renewal of the grace of Easter; by
taking part in it, we go with Christ through His
passion and death to the glory of His resurrection.

And, in each Sunday's Mass, we renew our joy in
sharing in the community of the Church, in the love
of the Spirit. Each Sunday we meet with our fellow

parishioners to hear the word of God, to pray together and together offer Christ's sacrifice, to be
bound more closely to one another in love by eating
the same Bread. Each Sunday's Mass should, then,
give us new courage and strength for the week ahead.
We should be alert to the passages in the Propers of
these Masses which remind us that in the Church
we share in the "mystery of Christ," living as children of the Father, in the Spirit.

These Masses also bring out the complementary
truth of our present miseries, weakness, danger from
our spiritual enemies. The Church is never unrealis-
tic, nor does she want us to be. She wants us to face
the facts of our present state; to remember that we
are in constant danger from the powers of evil, that
our life on earth must be a constant struggle. But the
point is that it need never be a hopeless struggle.
The mercy and strength of God are infinitely greater
than the cruelty and power of the devil; they are
greater than our own weakness and weariness. We
have only to "call out to the Lord"—as the Church
does in the chants of so many of these Masses—and
He will send us help.

These Masses bring out in various ways, especially
in the Epistles, the connection between our present
condition of human weakness and misery, and the
glorious life which is ours already because we are
Christ's members, the life which we now live by
faith and hope as well as love. Our Christian life is
meant to be a continual "passing-over," a transition,
a journey through sufferings and death to new and
fuller life. If Christ had not redeemed us, all the
troubles of human existence would be useless and

fruitless. But because He went through them all and so entered into His glory, we can go through them *with Him* to the same glory.

The Masses for these Sundays were not each planned as a whole as, for instance, were the Masses of Advent or Eastertime. The various parts of each Proper were brought together from various sources, and even the Epistle and Gospel do not closely correspond to one another. It is a mistake, therefore, to try to find any definite theme in any one of these Masses other than these general themes of the Christian life.

In general, however, it is well to remember, here as always, that the Epistle and the Gospel give God's message to us here and now. In the Epistle, Christ's messenger speaks to us, telling us, usually, of the practical effects that our participation in Christ's life should have in our daily lives. In the Gospel, the Lord Himself is speaking to us, by His words or by His actions. As St. Augustine says so beautifully: "The deeds of the Word are words to us." And St. Leo the Great states that "everything that was visible in our Redeemer's earthly life has passed into the sacraments." When, therefore, the Gospel shows our Lord teaching, feeding the multitude, healing a sick man, raising someone from the dead, calling His apostles, Christ is telling us not only what He did in the past, but also what He is doing here and now in the Church: teaching, healing, giving life, nourishing, calling and sending out His messengers. He is telling us what He will do for us in perfect fullness in heaven.

Again, in the chants of these Masses, as always, the Church, the Bride of Christ, is responding to the Word of God with the same Word. When we join in these chants, either by meditating them or actually singing, we are caught up into the song of the whole Church to the Lord whose return she is awaiting. By joining in these chants, we make our own the difficulties and dangers and sorrows and joys of her members all over the world. We are raised out of the narrow circle of our own interests and worries, we learn to pray as "catholics," that is, as people belonging to the universal Church, with the limitless scope of her interests, which are those of her Head.

Similarly, with the prayers of the Masses: the Collects, Secrets and Postcommunions. When we enter into them as the celebrant of the Mass prays them in our name, we are praying with and for the whole Church and all men. It will help our appreciation of these prayers if we take note of their structure and the function of each in the whole Mass.

The Collect is the prayer in which the celebrant gathers up, "collects," the personal prayers, the outpourings of the hearts of all present and offers the praise and petition of the whole Church to the Father, through Christ, in the Spirit. It usually begins with some words of praise and "confession" of God's majesty: "Almighty everlasting God. . . ." Frequently it contains a clause mentioning some wonderful work of God's on our behalf: "O God who. . . ." At other seasons of the year or on special feasts, this clause may mention one or other aspect of the redemption; here, in the Pentecost season, it is more general. These prayers thus follow the same plan as that of the great Eucharistic Prayer. We ask God, in virtue of what He has done already, to do still more, to complete His own work.

> O God, since you have prepared for those who love you such good things as eye has not seen: pour into our hearts the affection of your love, so that, loving you in all things and above all things, we may attain your promises which go beyond all desire, through our Lord Jesus Christ your Son, who lives and reigns with you in the unity of the Holy Spirit, God for ever and ever. Amen.

The Secret is, in the same way, the gathering up of the personal offerings of all present in the official offering prayer of the Church. Its text sometimes interprets the offerings as being the expression of our desire to make the Holy Sacrifice which is to follow our own sacrifice. It expresses the Church's prayer for the graces she desires from the Sacrifice. We can, therefore, learn a great deal about the Mass and our part in it by meditating on these prayers. For example, that of the Fifth Sunday: "Be moved, O Lord, by our supplications; and, in your kindness, accept these offerings of your servants; so that, what each one has offered to the honor of your name, may profit all to salvation. . . ."

The Postcommunion prayers ask that the grace of the Eucharist may wholly permeate our whole being, body and soul, our whole life and all our actions.

We can, then, learn a great deal from these prayers about the effects we should desire and pray for from our Communions, as well as how completely our Christian life should become "eucharized." For example, the marvelous Postcommunion for the Eleventh Sunday asks: "From the reception of thy sacrament, O Lord, may we feel your aid both in soul and body; so that, redeemed in both, we may glory in the abundance of the heavenly remedy." Or that for the Fifteenth Sunday: "May the working of the heavenly gift, we pray you, O Lord, take hold of us body and soul; so that not our own feeling, but the effect of the sacrament, may always prevail in us, through Jesus Christ our Lord. . . ."

With the Last Sunday after Pentecost, the Church looks forward to the final harvest, to the last day. Here all the themes of the liturgical year converge: fear of sin and our own weakness, fear of God's judgment; hope in His mercy and His love, for He has already rescued us from the power of darkness and transferred us into the kingdom of His beloved Son. And so we are ready to begin another Advent, looking forward to Christ's coming in grace and glory.

These weeks after Pentecost, then, are not meant to be merely marking time in our Christian life. Each Sunday offers us the graces we need, week by week, to "grow up in all things in Christ," not only for our own individual benefit, but for the glory of God and for the benefit of the whole Body of which we are members. Because of our growth in Christ during the summer-time, we should be readier to greet the Lord in the celebration of His coming next Christmas; and so readier to take part in the mystery of His death and resurrection next winter and spring. Taking part in the Church's program of instruction and formation and life-giving grace should more and more completely "Christen" us each year, so that when the Lord comes for us at death, and comes to all mankind on the last day, we shall be wholly His.

For study and discussion: What can we do to make the summertime a season of real growth in grace, not losing, but growing in the grace of the paschal celebration? How can we find or make time really to prepare for each Sunday's Mass, and to let its instructions and prayers echo in our lives during the following week, for the fuller fruition of its graces?

CHAPTER 13 DAYS OF
SPECIAL PRAYER,
EMBER DAYS,
THE GREAT
LITANY,
ROGATION DAYS

As we saw in the second chapter of this book, Christian prayer is, above all, the prayer of praise. Seen from our Lord's point of view, the celebration of the Eucharist is first of all a sacrifice of praise, which includes adoration and thanksgiving, although in God's infinite mercy it is also the sacrifice of our redemption. In the liturgy of the Mass, the aspect of praise is clearly stressed: "May the Lord receive this sacrifice at thy hands to the praise and glory of His Name," the assistants answer the celebrant when he asks them to pray that his sacrifice may be acceptable. And only after stressing this praise, do they go on to say, "to our own benefit and that of all His holy Church." At the beginning of the Canon, the Eucharistic Prayer, the celebrant again sums up what we are all going to do: *Let us give thanks to* (that is, praise and "confess," adore and thank) *the Lord our God.*

But, so long as we are pilgrims on earth—pilgrims who are really holy, members of Christ and His holy Church, whose praise of God is essentially the same as that of the angels and saints in heaven, but who at the same time are weak and in danger of falling into unholiness "seven times a day"—our praise must always be combined with the prayer of supplication, humbly asking for the things we need. Our Lord gave us the second part of the Our Father to follow on the first. He knew what we needed too well to teach us only the prayer of praise: "Hallowed be Thy Name, Thy kingdom come, Thy will be done . . ." but also, "give us this day our daily bread, forgive us . . . deliver us from evil."

The Church also recognizes our present state. Even on the greatest feasts of the year, praise of God and thanksgiving for the miracles of salvation He has wrought for us in His Son are combined with petition that we may live up to the graces He has given us, that we may be purified and strengthened. During the Easter vigil, at the *Exsultet,* it is true, the joy of the Church is so great that for a few moments she seems to forget that we are still only in the stage of anticipation and preparation. However, our long preparation for Easter, during pre-Lent and Lent, consists mainly in humbling ourselves before God and asking Him to have mercy on us.

Thus the Church gives us, in addition to the holy season of Lent, special "prayer days" during the year mainly devoted to supplication, to humbly asking God for His mercy and for everything else we need. Christ Himself taught us, in the Our Father and in many other places, to ask God for whatever we need.

Spiritual needs, mental needs, even our humblest physical needs are trustfully to be presented to our Father in Christ's Name. And not only in "private" prayers. The official liturgy of the Church includes these "prayers" also.

The *Ember Days* are of great antiquity in the Roman liturgy. The derivation of the English term is not entirely clear, but in Latin these are called *feriae quatuor temporum,* "the days of the four seasons," for they come at the beginning of each new season of the year. Each series of Ember Days includes the Wednesday and Friday of the week (in ancient times these were the week days for fasting and special services), and a celebration now held on Saturday morning which was originally a lengthy vigil service held during the night between Saturday and Sunday, ending in the offering of the Holy Sacrifice early Sunday morning.

This explains the lengthy series of Scripture readings in the Masses of the Ember Saturdays. Now there are five, but formerly there were not less than twelve! The Mass concluding the vigil was once itself the Sunday Mass, but when the vigil and its Mass was moved back, first to the evening and then to the morning before, special Propers for these Sundays were composed to fill the vacuum.

Someone has called the Ember Days the tri-monthly "days of recollection" in the liturgy. This term very clearly expresses for modern Christians the nature and purpose of these "days of the four seasons." The winter, summer and fall Ember Days are, first of all, echoes and reminders of the great

annual retreat of the Church, the holy season of
Lent. (The spring Ember days, which fall in Lent,
are thought to be a later addition, put in, as it were,
to complete the series. They seem to have been put in
the first week of Lent because this week has a very
pronounced penitential character.)

The lenten spirit of penance is, certainly, the main
feature of the Ember Days. The winter series falls
in the third week of Advent, and the Masses therefore contain the themes of this season. The Wednesday is often called "Golden Wednesday" and is in
many ways a celebration of the mystery of the Annunciation, while Friday gives the Gospel of the
Visitation. But the Secret of Wednesday is entirely
penitential: "May our fast be acceptable to thee, O
Lord, and in atoning for our sins, make us worthy
of thy grace. . . ." In the prayers of Saturday, Advent
and penitential themes combine; the thought of our
need for mercy and help continually recurs throughout all these Ember Days.

In the three other series—the spring Ember Days
in the first week of Lent, the summer ones during
Pentecost week, and the autumn series in September
—penance and the prayer of supplication are clearly
the main themes. But these expressions of our sinfulness and weakness are always, in each Ember Saturday Mass, concluded with the story from the book
of Daniel of the three young men in the fiery furnace
and their hymn of praise. This is one of the most
moving promises of the Resurrection of Christ and
of our redemption. And so we see that, while the
prayer of "asking" must follow on that of praise, it

also leads us to praise the God who surely answers our prayer.

Another theme is to be found in the liturgy of the Ember Days: our asking God to bestow His blessing on the crops of the earth and the land, and, in the autumn series, our thanking Him for them.[1] We are apt to feel that God does not have much to do with our supply of food in these days of modern science and technology, and that to pray to Him or thank Him for the "fruits" of the earth is rather superfluous and old-fashioned. But we should never let our preoccupation with all the "secondary causes" brought to our attention by science and technology obscure the primal fact that it is God who creates and provides and guides all things; that it is, finally, to Him that, as Psalm 103 says, "all creatures look for their food"; that it is He who is the final giver: "Thou dost open Thy hand and fill every living creature with thy blessing."

Finally, on the Ember Days, we pray for saintly and apostolic priests. According to Roman custom, the candidates for holy orders prepared themselves during these days, and received the orders from the bishop during the Saturday Vigil Service. Here again, we need to remember that whatever the human factors involved, and whatever the usefulness of "Vocation Days," etc., it is "God who gives the increase," who will give our young people, in answer to our earnest prayers, the impulse to serve Him heroically in all the ways of Christian life, so that "thy priests shall be clothed with justice and thy faithful shall shout for joy" (Psalm 31).

The other special "prayer days" in the liturgy
are of somewhat more recent origin. These are the
25th of April, the day of the "Major Litany," and
the three days before the feast of the Ascension, the
Rogation (or "asking") Days of the "Minor Litany." [2]

The celebration on April 25 originated in Rome;
it has been in existence at least since about 600 A.D.
This particular celebration is, certainly, of pagan
origin, for the Romans used to hold a procession
on this date to ask the god Robigus to protect the
crops against disease. The rite of The Litany is generally understood to be particularly a prayer for the
blessing and protection of the fruits of the earth—
see the Epistle for the Mass, which is the same as
that on the Rogation Days. But the petitions of
The Litany and the Mass Proper, both on April
25 and on the Rogation Days, have a much wider
reach: this is a day of supplication for all the needs
of the Church, of civil society, and of each human
being.

We call this great prayer—used on these "prayer
days" and, in a somewhat shortened form, during
the baptismal service of the Holy Easter night—the
"Litany of the Saints." But our calling upon the
members of the Church triumphant in heaven is
only a part of this prayer. After asking for the intercession of the saints, we go on to ask to be delivered
from all kinds of dangers; we implore God's mercy
because of the deeds that our Lord did for us, which
we enumerate with love; we ask for blessings for the
Church, the hierarchy, everyone on earth, and for
the faithful departed. The real name of this prayer
is simply *The Litany*. It is one of the most ancient

formulas in our prayer tradition; it has been used throughout Christian history on solemn prayer days and whenever any special danger threatened. For many centuries it was a dearly-loved daily prayer for the devout. We too could well learn to appreciate and pray it again as one of our own cherished "private prayers." The Our Father was given us by Christ Himself; we all love the "Hail Mary." But let us not forget that The Litany also belongs to the cherished treasure of traditional Catholic prayer.

For study and discussion: Study the September Ember-Day Masses. How do they bring out the various themes mentioned in this chapter? How could a three-day retreat be built on these Propers? What could be done to make the Ember Days real "days of recollection" in personal, family and parish observance? Study *The Litany.* How does it develop the various phrases of the Our Father? How does it teach us the blessings we should ask for?

NOTES

1 It is not certain whether or not the Ember Days originally had any connection with pagan fertility rites and the like. A few decades ago, scholars tended to find pagan influences in many observances of the Church; now they are more cautious. It is possible that the Church gave a Christian form to former pagan rites invoking the gods' protection on crops and so on. But the possibility of a biblical origin is also to be considered. The prophet Zacharias mentions fasting in Israel on the fourth, fifth, seventh and tenth months. (See the second and third readings of Pentecost Saturday, also the September readings.) Some modern scholars believe that the September Ember Days were connected in some way with the Jewish Feast of Tabernacles which, as

the second reading for the Saturday tells us, was established to remind Israel of the time when the people dwelt in tents in the desert, after the Lord rescued them from Egypt. This feast was also the anticipation of the blessings of the times of the Messiah, when once again the people would be completely the Lord's, nourished and cared for at His hand, living in the glory of His presence. Whatever the historical facts may be, all the Ember Days, and the September series in particular, should help us to see the creating power of God at work in all the fruitfulness of the earth, to realize the obligation on our part to do whatever we can to see that these fruits are distributed equitably to all men (note the frequent mention of justice to one another in the Ember-Day readings), and to realize also that all the blessings God gives to men in the "temporal order" are shadows and anticipations of the blessings He is preparing for us in His Kingdom.

2   The "Greater Litany" has, obviously, nothing to do with the feast of St. Mark; it is held on April 25 even when St. Mark's celebration is transferred to another day. Neither do the Rogation Days have any connection with the paschal season or the Feast of the Ascension. The Litany and procession on the Rogation Days were instituted by Bishop Mamertus of Vienne, in Gaul, about 470 A.D., at a time when the south of France was being visited by all sorts of calamities. Later on, this custom spread to other parts of the West, until finally, towards the end of the Middle Ages, it was definitely taken into the Roman liturgy. By then the meaning of these Rogation Days was taken to be the same as that of the Major Litany on April 25.

CHAPTER 14   **THE FEASTS
OF
OUR LORD**

So far in this book, we have been studying the feasts and seasons that make up the "Temporal Cycle" of the Church's year. As we have seen, this "cycle" forms, as it were, the spiral staircase by which year after year we climb toward the heavenly glory that the Father has prepared for those who believe in and follow His Son.

As we climb this staircase through the seasons of the year, the Church gives us also the various feasts that make up the "Cycle of the Saints." The purpose of all these feasts is to show us year by year more of the riches of the "mystery of Christ," of the life that the Father gives us through His Son in the Spirit, here and now and in the world to come; to give us the opportunity to praise and thank Him for them; and to enter more fully into them.

Most liturgical prayers are directed to the Father in heaven, the first Person of the Blessed Trinity.[1]

105

The Son and the Spirit are as eternal and infinite and perfect as the Father, but the Father is always named in the first place, and when the liturgy prays "O God . . ." it is usually the Father who is addressed. For He is the eternal principle of the Godhead; from Him the Son is eternally begotten as the Word which He speaks, the Wisdom expressing His Thought. From the Father and Son as the bond of Their eternal and unfathomable love the Holy Spirit proceeds. The wonder of our Christian life, as we saw in speaking about the feast of the Blessed Trinity, is that we have been drawn into this marvelous current of the inner life of God. We are "sons in the Son"; the Father has "sent the Spirit of His Son into our hearts," and in that Spirit we dare to cry out "Father."

Yet we do not know the Father directly. We know Him and we approach Him only through His Son made man. "No one knows the Father but the Son, and he to whom the Son chooses to reveal Him" (Matt. 11:27). "Philip, he who sees me, sees my Father also" (John 14:9). It is through Christ that we learn God's mercy and love. He is our only way to God; in Him alone is our salvation. Every liturgical prayer to the Father ends with the words "through Christ our Lord," to express our awareness of the wonderful privilege the Father has given us: to be able to pray to Him with and through His own Son, the Mediator through whom all God's gifts are given to us.

Thus the incarnate Son is always the center of the liturgy: He who is bringing us to the Father in the Spirit; He in whom the Father has "given us all good things"; our Redeemer, the head of the new Israel, the only priest and mediator, the victim of the Sacrifice, our teacher; our leader whenever we gather to pray; the revelation of God's infinite mercy; our never-failing strength, our example, the supreme judge of mankind, the pledge of our future glory and happiness.

All these aspects of the "mystery of Christ" are present in the celebration of the Holy Eucharist, and so, for some time in the early Church, there were very few special feasts other than the weekly celebration of our redemption each Sunday. As we saw in the first chapter, Easter Sunday was then singled out as the great annual celebration of the redemption, and gradually the whole paschal season and the preparation for it were developed to their present form. Then the Eastern and Western feasts of Christ's Birth, Epiphany and Christmas, were established, with a whole series of secondary celebrations. The most recent ones to be added to this series were those of our Lord's meeting Simeon in the Temple, on February 2 (now called Candlemas or the Purification of Our Lady), and that of His conception, on March 25. But since Jesus' Mother plays such an important part in both these mysteries, these are now named as feasts of the Blessed Virgin.

All these feasts were still not enough to satisfy faith and piety. Through the centuries, and in our own times, more feasts have been added, bringing out one or another aspect of the one "mystery of Christ." With one exception (May 3), these feasts are celebrated during the long "green season" between Pentecost and the beginning of Advent.

The first in the calendar, and also the earliest to be instituted, is that of May 3 in honor of *the Finding of the Holy Cross,* known in the Frankish kingdom even before the time of Charlemagne. Its Eastern counterpart, which we also now celebrate, is the Feast of *the Exaltation of the Holy Cross* on September 14. Both feasts began as commemorations of the finding and triumphant exhibition of the true cross, when, during the era of Constantine and St. Helena, the basilica of the Holy Sepulchre was built in Jerusalem. (September 14 was, apparently, the feast of the dedication of this church.) At the beginning of the seventh century, this holiest of relics, which had fallen into the hands of the pagan Persians, was brought back to Jerusalem by the Emperor Heraclius. This event gave a new significance to the feast of September 14.

In these two feasts, then, the Church invites us to enter into the spirit of Good Friday and venerate the cross "upon which hung the salvation of the world." But in these feasts we sing the joy there was not enough scope for on Good Friday. The cross, as the Introit sings, is the instrument of our salvation and resurrection, the instrument by which Our Lord merited to be exalted and to receive a Name above all names (Epistle), the victorious banner from which the enemies of God fly in fear (Communion).

The *Feast of the Precious Blood,* on July 2, might also be thought of as an echo of Good Friday. Blood is the symbol of the very life of a living creature. Our Lord gave His very life for us; He is the priest and victim of the Sacrifice which brings us into

God's presence and makes us share His life. And we share Christ's life by partaking of His body and blood in the Eucharist.

In the same way, the *Feast of Corpus Christi,* held during the week after the octave of Pentecost, is an echo of Holy Thursday. This feast was first instituted, during the Middle Ages, when devotion to the Blessed Sacrament began to develop. Later on, this same devotion found expression in the forms with which we are familiar. And when we study the vigorous and beautiful Proper of this feast (composed, tradition says, by St. Thomas Aquinas), we learn what all our devotion to the Blessed Sacrament should be like. Our Lord is sacramentally present on the altar, not to be "treasured" like a precious jewel or relic, but in the everyday form of bread to be eaten so that we may live by Christ as He lives by His Father (Gospel, also Introit, Gradual). This bread is the memorial of Christ's Passion (Collect and Epistle). Whenever we venerate it, we are venerating, "proclaiming" Christ's death and its dynamic effect in us. And we are looking forward to His return to bring us to share His glory, the glory of which our partaking of this Bread is the pledge and foretaste (Collect and Postcommunion).

After the cycle of the great feasts of our salvation, a week after Corpus Christi comes the *Feast of the Sacred Heart,* showing us that everything that our Lord did and suffered for us was done out of love, the divine human love of the incarnate Son. It is in Christ's love that the love of God is revealed and given to us (Collect); His infinite mercies, the eternal thought of God in our regard, are revealed to us in Christ (Introit, Alleluia, Epistle). And the love of the incarnate Son for His Father (Easter Offertory, Secret) is the exemplar of the love that should be ours as Christ's members.

To use the human heart of our Lord, pierced on the cross, as the symbol and summary of the infinite generosity of God toward us, of the love of Christ for His Father and for us, is indicated by Holy Scripture itself (Gospel). The modern developments of devotion to the Sacred Heart, rightly understood, only bring out various aspects of the perennial faith and devotion of the Church. Each *First Friday* reminds us that "Love is His meaning," as a medieval English mystic once put it, in everything that He did and does for us. Our devotion to His love on First Fridays should take its special color and motive from the liturgical season.

The *Feast of the Transfiguration of Our Lord* on August 6 is one of the greatest feasts in the calendar of the Eastern Churches, and has been celebrated in the West since the end of the Middle Ages. It is an echo and development of the Second Sunday in Lent, when the Gospel presents us with the same mystery. Even before His Resurrection, Our Lord revealed to the three apostles who were to witness His agony the glory of His God-manhood. The Father Himself proclaims His Son as the teacher of His eternal wisdom, covered with the bright cloud of the Spirit. The splendor and wonder of this single glimpse of Christ's glory shines out in the Epistle written by one of the "eyewitnesses of His majesty." In the mystery of this feast, we realize not only Christ's glory, but our own hope of sharing it as adopted children and co-heirs with Him (Collect).

On the last Sunday of October, we celebrate the *Feast of Christ the King,* instituted by Pope Pius XI not so many years ago. The idea is as old as the Church. Christ's Kingship was foretold and foreshadowed in the Old Testament (Introit Psalm, Gradual, and Alleluia, Offertory, Communion verse) and proclaimed in the New (Gospel, Epistle). This is the theme of the Feast of the Epiphany and the whole Epiphany season. But since it had hardly any place in modern Catholic thought, this new feast was instituted to bring it once more within the focus of our thinking and our piety. The Collect shows us the meaning of Christ's Kingship in relation to society today, and the Preface gives a marvelous summary of the whole design of our salvation and the purpose of human history: the final establishment of Christ's kingdom of "truth and life, of justice, love and peace."

Another series of feasts should be mentioned here, those of the *Dedication of Churches.* If our parish church has been consecrated (not all are, since there are stringent conditions to be fulfilled before this may be done), then the anniversary of its consecration or dedication is one of the major celebrations of the year for us. And the whole Church celebrates the anniversaries of the dedication of the great basilicas of St. John Lateran (Nov. 9) and of St. Peter's and St. Paul's-outside-the-Walls (November 18).[2]

Here, too, the "mystery of Christ" is the center of the celebration. The fact that He comes to dwell

among us, in a house we have made, as He came
into the house of Zachaeus (Gospel) is the pledge
of His bringing us to dwell with Him in the city
of God in heaven. Thus the church building is,
above all, the token in our midst of the eternal
Jerusalem in heaven. The holiness of God's house
is praised with the words Holy Scripture uses to
describe the glory of God's temple above (Introit,
Epistle). The keynote of this relationship is found in
the final sentence of the Epistle: "Behold, I make all
things new." In our parish church, in every church,
Christ is, here and now, making all things new, by
the celebration of the Eucharist and the administration of the sacraments, in preparation for the final
"making new" when He comes again in glory.

For study and discussion: What are some of the reasons
why most of these feasts of Our Lord are placed in the
summer-autumn season of the liturgical year? How does
the use of texts from the Old Testament in these Masses
help us to understand the New Testament? The feast
we are celebrating? Our own Christian life? How does
each of these feasts help us to make a more complete
picture of our Lord's work? How does it help us to come
to know Him better?

NOTES

1   Of course, we also pray to the Blessed Trinity as such,
when we recite the "Glory be to the Father . . ." for instance. Especially during Pentecost week, our prayers are
directed to the Holy Spirit. And in the liturgy we also often
pray directly to Christ our Lord. This is not a recent development, as once used to be claimed; parts of very ancient
hymns, like the *Gloria* now in the Mass, or the *Te Deum*,
are directed to Christ. And the acclamation *Kyrie, eleison*

used in all litanies and at the beginning of Mass, is often explained as a prayer to the incarnate Son in His glory.

2 Other feasts of the sanctoral cycle also originated as anniversaries of dedications of churches. The best known are those on August 5 (St. Mary Major in Rome), and September 29 (St. Michael). In these cases, the Masses used are not that of the dedication, but of devotion to the mystery or the patron saint.

CHAPTER 15   THE FEASTS
OF THE
HOLY MOTHER
OF GOD

FROM THE VERY BEGINNING, Jesus' holy Mother has
been held in high honor. Whenever the great writers of the Church have been dealing with the mystery of the Incarnation, they have spoken of Mary.
The fact that Christ had a mother "according to the
flesh" shows that He is really man, really one of our
race, the "Son of David" and of all His human fore-
bears. But the fact that this mother is truly the
Mother of God—the doctrine formulated at the
Council of Ephesus—means that her Child is He
who can truly save us from our sins. Mary's most
ancient and most fitting title is, then, "Mother of
God." None of the later ones like Our Lady, Notre
Dame, Madonna, are so expressive as this.

But the fact that she was Jesus' Mother "according to the flesh" did not play the major part in the
development of devotion to her. Holy Scripture
gives us, in the words of Elizabeth at the Visitation,
114

the reason why Mary is "blessed among women": "Blessed art thou because thou hast believed." This is why the Gospel read in the Masses of many of her feasts repeats the words of our Lord, "Blessed are they who hear the word of God and keep it." For Mary is "the faithful one" par excellence. By her faith and obedience she undid the harm caused by the disobedience of the first Eve. She is the greatest daughter of Abraham, "the father of all who believe." She is the personification of Israel, in whom mankind met its Savior (Magnificat). And so she is the type of the New Israel, the Church; she is its protectress, and the model of all the faithful, and their Mother.

The leading themes of all her feasts and of the writings of the Fathers about her are, then: God's special choice of her for this unique place in His plan for our salvation, and the exceptional holiness with which she responded to her calling. We might say that all the various ways in which we call upon her as Mother of God stress the first aspect, and those calling her the Virgin of Virgins mainly express the second.

This is why the expression in the liturgy of devotion to Mary always emphasizes the close relationship between the mysteries of our Lord and the vocation and wonderful holiness of His Mother. Her feasts are best understood as a kind of echo of His. For she is, as it were, the Christian *par excellence,* the one in whom Christ's redeeming work met no shadow of opposition, but the fullness of human cooperation. This also explains why the earliest commemorations of Jesus' Mother in the Roman liturgy are related to Christmas. The Gospel of the Annunciation is read on Ember Wednesday in Advent, and later also on the following Sunday. Some scholars think that the commemoration of the octave day of Christmas (the prayers for the present Feast of the Circumcision) are an early phase of the same liturgical development. These are, however, not feasts in the proper sense.

The earliest feasts in honor of the blessed Mother of God all originated in the Christian East. In the course of the seventh century, they were introduced into Rome, probably by Popes from the East already familiar with them. These most ancient feasts of Mary are those of February 2, March 25, August 15, and September 8.

The first two, the Feast of the Purification and that of the Annunciation, are, properly, feasts of our Lord. But the Greeks had already emphasized the important part of Mary in these mysteries, and today we think of them almost entirely as celebrations in her honor.

The feast of February 2 is the final feast of the Christmas cycle. Most of the texts of the Mass itself refer to our Lord who, for the first time, in obedience to the law, came into the temple and was recognized by holy Simeon. It is because Simeon called Him "the light to enlighten the nations and the glory of thy people, Israel," that candles are blessed and carried in procession on this day, and that it received its popular name of "Candlemas." During the procession the Church more particularly honors Jesus' Mother, especially in the beautiful antiphon taken from the Greek: "Adorn thy bridal chamber

. . . greet Mary with loving embrace, for she who is the very gate of heaven brings thee the glorious King of the new light."

The feast of March 25 was meant in the first place as a celebration of the Incarnation, of the conception of our Lord. In some early documents it is called the feast of "Mary's Conceiving," and soon came to be thought of as the celebration of the mystery of the annunciation to her of her vocation and of her acceptance of it, so that "the Word was made flesh." The Proper of the Mass is all in honor of the Virgin Mother and contains the earliest texts used in Rome for the feasts of Mary. The Lesson gives the prophecy: "Behold a Virgin shall conceive and bear a Son"; the Gospel the story of the angel's message and Mary's response. And the chants use the royal marriage-psalm, 44, to sing her praises.

The most important among all the feasts of the Mother of God always has been, and still is, that of her *Assumption* into heaven (August 15). In her the glory of the Resurrection has already been realized. Already she shares, body and soul, in the glory of her Son. In praising her, we wonder at the fullness of glory which will be given to all redeemed mankind at the last day. Here, too, she is the type of the Church and the model of all her children: where she is, we all hope one day to be. She is enthroned in heaven as a pledge of the future splendor of the whole Church, and also as the protectress who is never invoked in vain.

In the Proper for this feast, the Church invites us to look at the Virgin Mother, the woman who, as St. John saw on Patmos, appears both as a sign in the heavens and as the Church in its final glory, of which she is the type (Psalm and Antiphon of the Introit). Mary is the true Judith (Epistle) who overcame the enemy of mankind, who is the glory and joy of her people, the new Israel. In her, the work of salvation has been fully and gloriously realized. That is why we call her blessed (Gospel and Communion) and pray that, through her intercession, we too may share in the glory of Christ's Resurrection (prayers).

Among the more recent Eastern feasts borrowed by the Latin Church, the most important is that of Mary's Conception, December 8, called since the solemn definition of the doctrine by Pius IX in 1854 by the name which Christian piety had given it for centuries, *The Immaculate Conception*. Throughout the centuries, theologians and devout Christians had been aware of the fact that the beginning of Mary's existence in the womb of her mother was the "dawn of salvation" in a special sense. In order to become the Mother of God, Mary was preserved, by the merits of the Savior she was to bear as her Child, from all guilt and stain of sin (Collect). In her, creation, contaminated by sin, returned to its primal innocence.

This is why a Lesson from the book of Proverbs, read also on the feast of Mary's birth, September 8, is used in the Mass for this feast. Mary is God's purest creature, the realization of the eternal plan of God's Wisdom, according to which God created the world and mankind to be a mirror of His eternal perfection. In this and many other of her feasts and commemorations (the Saturday Masses in her honor, for instance) passages are read from this same book of Scripture describing God's timeless Wisdom, the pattern of the first creation and also of the successive realities in which the new creation takes place: Israel, Mary, the Church.

Many other feasts of the Mother of God adorn the liturgical year, each bringing out some aspect of her motherhood and her holiness, her unique place in the Church and its history. The same themes run through them all, developed in various ways: God's choice of Mary for her unique role; her marvelous and perfect response in faith and obedience. As we come to each of these feasts, let us notice how the Church rejoices in the glories of the Mother of God, praising her, and praising God for her. And let us take part in this praise, while asking that, by her intercession, we may grow more like her in faith and obedience and attain to the joys of everlasting life.

Suggestions for study and discussion: How are the themes mentioned in this chapter developed in the Saturday Masses, in the Common for feasts of the Mother of God, in some of her feasts throughout the year? How might our personal, family, and parish devotion to her be nourished and strengthened by the use of some of these texts?

CHAPTER 16　　**THE FEASTS**
OF
THE SAINTS

THE "MYSTERY OF CHRIST," as we saw earlier, is the center of everything the Church does. This is true of the "Temporal Cycle" of the liturgical year, of the other feasts of our Lord which have been added during the centuries, of those in honor of His Blessed Mother, and also of those of the saints. Christ Himself taught us the true foundation of all devotion to the holy ones in heaven: "If anyone serves me, let him follow me, and where I am, there also shall my servant be; if anyone serves me, my Father will honor him" (John 12:26).

The saints were true followers of Christ; in them we are able to recognize the features of our Savior. Because of their likeness to His Son, the Father has admitted them to the eternal kingdom where they share the glory of the risen Lord. Therefore, they are our models, and they have been given the power to intercede for us. They are our brothers and sisters in Christ; the prayers of the liturgy take the fact of their interest in us and their intercession for us for granted. These prayers only ask that God may make their intercession fruitful for us: for the forgiveness of our sins, for our growth in faith and devotion, for our joining their company in heavenly joy. When St. Therese said that she would "spend her heaven in doing good upon earth," she was expressing a fundamental conviction of Catholic faith, that the holy ones in heaven, who have arrived at their goal, want to help us in every way to follow Christ as they did.

The veneration of the saints is always closely associated with the celebration of the Holy Eucharist. The one Sacrifice, offered once and for all on Calvary and remaining present among us on the altar, is the source of their glory in heaven. This is clearly brought out, for example, in the Secret of the Mass on feasts of confessor bishops, *Sacerdotes tui:* "May the yearly feast of your holy confessor and bishop make us acceptable to your loving kindness; and may the service of loving atonement with which we keep it earn for him increase of glory and win us the gifts of your grace." On the other hand, because of their heavenly glory, they are able to be our intercessors with God and to make the gifts we offer acceptable to Him: "May the loving prayer of thy Saint fail us not, O Lord, and may it render our offerings acceptable to thee" (Secret of the Mass *In medio*).

Finally, the feasts of the saints are to give us joy: "O God, who dost gladden us by the yearly celebration of the feast of blessed N. . . ." The fact that they

are already in the glory of heaven is a pledge of
God's love for those who believe in His Son. Because they, men and women like ourselves, have followed Christ through His passion and cross to the
glory of His resurrection, we dare to lift up our eyes
from our present troubles, to be glad for their happiness, and to hope that one day we may share it
also.

All the saints are followers of Christ, and yet each
group has its special pattern of holiness, its particular way of carrying out the imitation of Christ which
is the essence of all sanctity. These various patterns
can easily be discerned in the traditional liturgy, as
can be seen most clearly in the short series of Masses
called the Common of the Saints, made up of
various parts taken from the most ancient Masses for
saints' days and used on feasts for which the Missal
provides no special Proper.

The first in this series is the Mass for Holy Popes.
This Proper was added recently, by Pius XII; prior
to this time, if there was no special formulary, the
Common of a Martyr-Bishop or of a Confessor-
Bishop was used. This new Mass emphasized the vocation of St. Peter and his successors to be the rock
on which the Church is built. So the texts praise
the saintly fortitude and firmness with which they
exercised their exalted function, completely devoted
to their task, with no self-seeking, in great humility
(Epistle).

The liturgical veneration of the saints began with
the cult of the martyrs, whose Masses come next in
the Common of the Saints. During the centuries of
persecution, they were the only saints honored by a

liturgical celebration. Their fellow-Christians carefully recorded the dates of their martyrdom, of their "birthday" as the liturgy calls it, on which they were born into heavenly glory. The word "martyr" means "witness"; they were seen to be true followers of Christ, carrying out in a most perfect way His command to "witness" to Him, doing so by giving up their lives as He had done. And when the age of persecutions was over, the first confessors to be venerated as saints—like St. Anthony in the East and St. Martin in the West—were considered to have attained holiness because their life of prayer and penance had constituted an unbloody martyrdom.

The Propers for the feasts of many early martyrs (such as those of the beloved Roman martyrs, St. Lawrence and St. Agnes) belong to the most ancient parts of the Sanctoral Cycle. From these formularies, the various texts were taken for the Masses for the Common of Martyrs. The key-note of all these Masses is found in the Gospels: "He who does not take up his cross and follow me . . . who does not renounce all that he possesses. . . ." "If anyone wishes to come after me, let him deny himself. . . . He who loses his life for my sake will find it." "Everyone who acknowledges me before men, him will I acknowledge before my Father who is in heaven." The Epistles and the chants sing the praises of these men who so perfectly followed Christ.

These praises are especially joyful on the feast of a martyr-bishop, as representing, so to speak, the perfect union of official and personal, "objective" and "subjective" sanctity. As a bishop, he represented Christ in the Church; as a martyr, he became in an even more perfect way like to Him who became our High Priest by His passion and death.

Thinking along these lines, we begin to arrive at a deeper understanding of the glory of martyrdom. We understand also why, during the paschal season when we are celebrating the salvation accomplished by our Lord in His Passion and revealed to us in His risen glory, there is a special Common for Martyrs. They are the truly fruitful branches of the vine which is Christ; they "abided in Him," even to sharing His suffering and death. Therefore they live forever in His love and His joy is fulfilled in them (Gospels of the Commons of Martyrs for Eastertime).

"Confessor" was originally a synonym for "martyr," meaning one who "confessed," or, as we would say, "professed" or witnessed to the true God and His incarnate Son. As was said above, after the period of persecution, this title was given to those who followed our Lord by lives of penance and prayer, although they were not given the opportunity actually to become martyrs. In the Masses, a distinction is made between the confessors who were bishops—that is, successors of the apostles, "sent" to their flocks by Christ as He was sent by the Father, chosen official representatives of Christ as priest, teacher, and pastor—and the confessors who were not bishops. (No distinction is made between those who were priests or deacons and those who were not, on the principle that it is only a bishop who fully represents Christ in the various functions of His priesthood.)

In honor of these holy bishops, the Church has us sing the praises of the high priests of old, and of David the chosen King, who foreshadowed the one "eternal priest according to the order of Melchisedech," the promised Ruler of His people, and those who represent Him on earth.

There is also a special Mass for doctors, that is, teachers, of the Church, and for holy abbots. The doctors were "filled with the spirit of wisdom and understanding" (Introit); they are the salt of the earth, who both taught and carried out God's commandments, and are therefore called "great" in the kingdom of heaven (Gospel). And the holy monks are venerated especially because they "meditated on the law of the Lord"; like Moses, they taught the law of life and wisdom and therefore are among the saints in glory (Epistle).

But the keynote of all these Masses for confessors is the same: it is given us in the Gospels, in the parable about the faithful servant who will be given authority over all the goods of his master, who is invited to "enter into the joy of his Lord," and in Christ's words about all those who have left everything for His sake and who will receive a hundredfold and life everlasting.

The Masses for the feasts of holy women are among the most beautiful in the whole Missal. Here again, the most expressive texts from the Propers of early liturgical formularies have been brought together in these Commons. One striking characteristic is that there is very little difference between the Masses for virgin martyrs and those for women martyrs who were not virgins. And even in the Common for a Holy Woman who was neither a virgin nor a martyr, we find many texts taken from the Masses for holy virgins. One Gospel, used only on the feast of a virgin, is the Lord's parable about the five wise virgins who faithfully awaited the coming of the bridegroom. Another, used also on the feasts of other holy women, speaks of a "treasure hidden in a field," a "pearl of great price," which take all one's substance to acquire. Here is the basic truth about the lives of all the holy women venerated by the Church, whatever their path of life. Nothing spectacular: the hidden existence of giving everything day by day for the treasure, the love of Christ; of awaiting, not idly but in prudent preparedness, for the coming of the Lord. This is why they are called "wise" and why the Church sings in their honor the verses of Psalm 44 which speak of the beauty of the queen placed in honor at the right hand of the king.

Once a year, on November 1, we celebrate a feast in honor of all the saints in heaven, those publicly acknowledged as such by the Church and all the "great multitude" whose names are not known on earth. (Who knows, among them may be our own relatives, our friends and former neighbors!) On this day, the liturgy gives us no special pattern of holiness; instead we listen to the words of the Lord describing the essential lines of all holiness: blessed are the poor in spirit . . . the meek . . . the clean of heart. . . .

We should at least mention here the feasts of those

saints who, like the Mother of God herself, were in a special way intimately connected with the work of our salvation. St. John the Baptist has two feasts —that of his birthday (June 24) and of his martyrdom (August 29). He had the great vocation of being the last and the greatest of all the prophets, the immediate forerunner of Christ, chosen to "prepare his way before Him." He is the link between the Old Testament and the New, sanctified in his mother's womb as a special servant of God, the "friend of the bridegroom" who proclaimed Christ present among His people, who died a martyr, witnessing to the truth.

Then there are the feasts of the apostles, the foundation stones of the Church which is the "Temple to God in the Spirit." Every feast has its own Proper, but the key-note of them all is that these are the honored friends of the Lord, faithful to His charge. They take the place of their forefathers after whom the tribes of Israel were named; they are the princes and judges of the new Israel, the people of God all over the world, through all centuries.

St. Joseph also was very close to our Lord. His important role in the mystery of our Lord's early years on earth is, apart from the flight into Egypt, buried in obscurity. In the liturgical tradition of the Church, no special feast was set apart for him until the end of the Middle Ages. But today we have two feast-days: 1) on March 19, celebrating him as the great saint whom God "set over His household," the "just man," as St. Matthew calls him, which, in biblical language, means a man of outstanding holiness; 2) on May 1, we celebrate the new feast of St. Joseph the Worker, honoring him especially for the example he gave us all of the hard and hidden work of ordinary living made into a means of following Christ to the heights of holiness.

The Liturgy of the Faithful Departed

In every Mass, during the Canon, the Church prays for "those who have gone before us with the sign of faith and who sleep the sleep of peace . . . to them, O Lord, and to all who rest in Christ, grant, we pray, the place of refreshment, of light and of peace."

These words give us the themes of all the special Masses and prayers for the "faithful departed." Those who have not yet entered into heavenly joy need our prayers to help prepare them to go into the glory of heaven, yet already they are in peace, certain of their salvation, aware of God's infinite mercy and love. The Propers of the liturgy for the dead are, above all, characterized by hope in God's infinite mercy and in the infinite power of Christ's redemption. Once death led only to the world "below," to darkness and terror. Since our Lord went through death to life, we believe that all those marked with the "sign of faith," that is, of baptism, who died in union with Christ, will be brought safely through the shadows of death to His peace and light and life, to the companionship of all the saints, with Him, in the presence of the Father.

By far the greater part of the liturgical texts express this theme, that Christ is the resurrection and the life. In the Propers, only the Dies Irae and the

Offertory give the note of fear—terror of the "deep pit" and the "lion's mouth," and of the Day of Wrath at the end of the world. These texts, it is true, are of later origin than the rest. And yet we need them too. For, while the Masses for the Dead are, primarily, offered for the repose of the souls of the departed, the texts are also for us. And we need to be reminded of the "fear of the Lord" which is the beginning of wisdom, the need for never-failing obedience to God's law, as well as to be led to think of His eternal mercy and of the joy of the eternal home He has prepared for us in heaven.

To pray for the dead is no mechanical exercise to be gone through in a routine way. It is a sacred duty, incumbent on each of us, for the faithful departed are our brothers and sisters in the Communion of Saints, already close to God. As they desire to be united with Him in happiness forever, to praise Him in His presence, so we should desire this for them, and offer our prayers with the Church that they may speedily attain it.

For study and discussion: The Communion of Masses for the dead asks that they may share the companionship of the saints. Do we think of life in heaven as one of companionship with the holy men and women we most venerate? How would a study of the Commons of the saints and of the Proper Masses for the dead make our ideas about eternal life more vivid and concrete? Our ideas about Christian life here and now?

NOTE

1   The "eternal rest" so frequently asked for the dead in liturgical prayers does not mean doing nothing, but rather has the idea of happy activity, free from the weariness and frustration and pressure of work on earth, the activity of praise and communication in love proper to the eternal holy day, the "Sabbath rest" of the Lord. Similarly, "light" has all the connotations given by Scripture and the liturgy; "peace" means the fullness of the blessings of Messianic times, described in terms of earthly prosperity and happiness by the prophets of old. And "refreshment" is another way of expressing in human terms these realities which "eye has not seen and ear has not heard, nor has it entered into the heart of man to conceive, what things God has prepared for those who love Him."